PENGUIN

FOCUS ON
WHAT MATTERS

Darius Foroux (pronounced as Da-reeus Fo-roo) is the author of 7 books, and the creator of 6 online courses. He writes about productivity, business, Stoicism, and wealth building. His ideas and work have been featured in TIME, NBC, Fast Company, Inc., Observer, and many more publications. Until now, more than 30 million people have read his articles.

FOCUS ON WHAT MATTERS

A Collection of Stoic Letters on Living Well

DARIUS FOROUX

PENGUIN BOOKS

An imprint of Penguin Random House

PENGUIN BOOKS

USA | Canada | UK | Ireland | Australia
New Zealand | India | South Africa | China | Singapore

Penguin Books is part of the Penguin Random House group of companies
whose addresses can be found at global.penguinrandomhouse.com

Published by Penguin Random House India Pvt. Ltd
4th Floor, Capital Tower 1, MG Road,
Gurugram 122 002, Haryana, India

Penguin
Random House
India

First published in Penguin Books by Penguin Random House India 2023
Copyright © Darius Foroux 2022

All rights reserved

10 9 8 7 6

The views and opinions expressed in this book are the author's own and
the facts are as reported by him/her which have been verified to the extent
possible, and the publishers are not in any way liable for the same.

ISBN 9780143461845

Printed at Gopsons Papers Pvt. Ltd., Noida

This book is sold subject to the condition that it shall not, by way of trade
or otherwise, be lent, resold, hired out, or otherwise circulated without the
publisher's prior consent in any form of binding or cover other than that in
which it is published and without a similar condition including this condition
being imposed on the subsequent purchaser.

www.penguin.co.in

MIX
Paper from
responsible sources
FSC® C191020

INTRODUCTION

I discovered Stoicism in early 2015, right around the time my grandmother passed away, and I was dealing with a breakup *and* a career switch—everything happened at the same time. Stoicism helped me remain resilient during that difficult time. I've been studying the philosophy ever since. Roughly speaking (and highly generalizing), there are two philosophies on which to base your life.

1. **Seeking pleasure:** Think of Hedonism and some ideas from Epicureanism.

2. **Finding pleasure in duty:** Think of Stoicism, Zen, and other philosophies that promote self-reliance.

I believe seeking pleasure is the current philosophy of the world. We live in a society that revolves around pleasure, consumption, and escapism. Most of us simply want to be comfortable in life. While there's nothing wrong with making our lives better, there's a major risk in taking this philosophy too far. When you're primarily driven by pleasure, you risk ending up on the hedonic treadmill. This is not new information. We all know social media makes us feel unworthy and depressed. We know we can't buy our way to happiness. We also know that seeking pleasure turns us into slaves of our desires. And yet, we fall for these traps every day.

One of my favorite Stoic philosophers is Seneca. He was not only a thinker, but he also had a long career in politics, serving as a senator and later as the advisor to Nero. His works show how practical he was. Toward the end of his life, he started traveling and writing letters to his friend, Lucilius.

The goal of these letters was to share Stoic thoughts with Lucilius, who had hedonistic tendencies and lived a busy life. At the time, Seneca himself took a step back from public life and left Rome. From the quiet countryside of southern Italy, he wrote 124 letters to Lucilius. I've been a long-time fan of these. You can tell that Seneca subtly tries to convince his friend to be more stoic, to pursue tranquility, and to focus on what's inside his control.

Seneca's original letters still serve as reminders to focus on the right things in life. The Stoics believed that to live a happy life, you need to go against the herd. In a letter to his brother, Seneca wrote this:

> **"Let us enquire what is the best, not what is the most customary, thing to do, and what establishes our claim to unending happiness."**

I love Seneca's letters to his friend because it feels like he could've written them to you and me, living in the 21st century. Seneca successfully stepped away from the busy life of Rome and gave Lucilius an outside perspective. Sometimes, that's all you need to get out of your own head. Inspired by Seneca's renowned letters, I started writing a weekly in 2020 that I called the Stoic Letter.

Focusing on what we can control doesn't mean detaching or running away from the world's daily realities. It's all about balance. And being more proactive instead of reactive. To have that clarity, I've divided the letters into two parts:

1. **The Inner World:** Everything related to mastering your own mind.

2. **The Outer World:** Everything related to becoming the master of your own destiny.

While many of us desire to become the rulers of our destiny, we can't embark on that endeavor unless we master our inner world first. Otherwise, we will give up every time we experience a setback. To me, living well is about having a balance between having inner peace and finding success in our careers and lives. When those two things collide, we find a deep sense of meaning. In this book, you will read letters on nearly every topic on the mind of a person who's trying to live well. That period also signifies one of the most mentally challenging times of our lives. We've been going through a lot of changes in the world since then.

I must admit that it's much harder to stay focused and peaceful now, compared to before 2020. That's not just something people say. It's true. That's why I wrote these letters. After receiving so much good feedback, I decided to publish them as a collection. My goal is that these letters help you focus on the things that matter most in life. The things that *you* value—not the herd. Read the book as you please: From cover to cover or simply skip to the topics that are relevant to you.

Enjoy!

-Darius

P.S. Throughout the book you'll find illustrations at the end of some of the letters. I've created this together with my illustrator to visualize the main idea of the letter.

I.

THE INNER WORLD

All improvement starts within. We can't be happy and comfortable in the world if we are not the same in our minds. But being happy and having peace of mind is a difficult task in our distracted world. As soon as we find mental balance and we feel somewhat content, something happens that shakes us to the core.

With Stoic wisdom, we can guard our minds against the things that disrupt our happiness. When you apply the strategies from the Stoics, you will become mentally tougher, which will in turn give you more tranquility. A strong mind is a peaceful mind.

MANAGING YOUR EMOTIONS

"Understand at last that you have something in you more powerful and divine than what causes the bodily passions and pulls you like a mere puppet."

— Marcus Aurelius

LETTER 1:
ON KNOWING
WHAT YOU CONTROL

It's so important to only focus on what you control. Everyone seems to talk about that when life is difficult, which is great because we all need those types of reminders. But I also feel like I'm constantly bombarded with useless information, which neutralizes those good reminders. This morning I saw something about Bitcoin, and then I spent the next thirty minutes following one link after the other. I started reading about the history of money, but by the end, I was getting lost on Wikipedia. How often does this happen to you? You start with watching a video, then you look something up, and soon you're down a rabbit hole of useless information.

What I learned from Stoicism is that time is your most valuable resource.

Maybe it's nice to know about everything in the world, but there's no way we can actually use all the information we consume. So these pursuits are largely a waste of time. I will never get back the time I spent hopping from one Wikipedia page to the next one. We all need to be more conscious of how we spend our time. Most of us know this—we just don't live it. We squander our time like it's nothing.

We read articles about how bad the world is, we browse the social media profiles of our ex-partners, we watch TV shows we're not even interested in just to "kill time." Why kill something so precious? That's what should really upset you. Not some insignificant message you read on Twitter from some person you don't even know. We're all so quick to get triggered by others. Why do we feel the need to respond to every single thing that we run into? We don't control what other people say or do.

Without accepting that we don't control most things in life, we can never have lasting happiness. Getting concerned with things outside of our control is a habit.

There will always be some kind of national or international issue to worry about. Whether it's a recession, war, natural disaster, protest, or social issue, you can't escape bad things. It's good to practice indifference to things that are outside of your control but do impact your happiness.

What actually matters to your happiness? Good friendships, work that you enjoy, reading books that make you think, walking in nature, working out, watching a good movie—you know this. Last Saturday, I woke up, did some reading and writing, had brunch with my family, then went for a walk together, came back, did some more writing and reading, had dinner, and watched a movie in the evening. It was a good day.

It's a stark contrast with another day I had last week. I was talking to another friend about COVID. I got a bit carried away. "They just got to shut down the whole world for 3 weeks and we're done!" That didn't happen earlier this year, and it's obviously not going to happen now. I kept that negative energy with me during the day and guess what I did? Not much. I just consumed more useless information. I didn't create anything useful that day. Things are the way they are, and we need to deal with them. That's how it's been for the past 10,000 years, and probably will be for the next 10,000. What happens after that? No one knows, not even the world's most famous futurist, Elon Musk. Getting just a little bit heated over COVID was a waste of my energy and didn't make anything better for anyone. Our best bet is to make our own lives better—NOW.

Start the circle small. Go to bed a bit stronger— mentally and physically. Help your partner, kids, parents, siblings, friends, and expand the circle like that. I see it as a sequential thing.

Start with yourself, and then expand your reach, one person at a time.

We probably won't get old enough to expand the circle to the world. But hey, it's pretty good if you can make your own life and the lives of the people you care about better. That's already hard enough. Just don't make things harder by wasting time on things you don't control. Know what you can and cannot control! That's the Stoic's path to a happy life.

If you set a high value on happiness, everything else must be valued less.

LETTER 2:
ON PROTECTING YOUR MOOD

Have you noticed how you often absorb someone else's energy? You might wake up excited and joyful. You start singing as you wait for your coffee. You have a great breakfast, go to your work, and just enjoy your life. In the evening, you meet a friend. And when you meet each other, your friend seems depressed for some reason. You just notice it through their body language and sad voice.

And all of a sudden, you feel the energy inside you shifting. You forget about the joy you experienced throughout the day. You also get a bit down. Your friend asks, "How was your day?" And you say, "Same old, same old."

You actually wanted to say, "My day was GREAT! Really had a good time today."

This is a common event in life. We're all sensitive to signals we get from others. And this is also true the other way around. Others can also be influenced by your mood. When two moods collide, one usually wins, and it's often the negativity because it's such a powerful energy. Now, what can you do about this? Some people are committed to avoiding negativity at all costs. They only want to be surrounded by positivity. This is not a realistic desire. It's the same as saying, "I want to be healthy but I don't want to work out."

The Stoics had a great way to deal with this issue. They believed in being compassionate, but remaining cautious of another person's energy. To a Stoic, their own sanity is more important than feeling someone else's pain. But that doesn't mean they were distant or cold.

Here's what Epictetus said: "You may see people who are distraught and in tears because they had to part with their child or lost some material possession. Don't let the impression lead you to think that something bad happened to them. They are not upset by what happened to them but by their view of the situation. However, be careful not to show disdain for their grief. Show them sympathy, use comforting words, and even share their misery outwardly. But make sure that you do not inwardly grieve with them."

You can be there for someone, show sympathy, and express your understanding. But as a Stoic, you should never forget what's correct judgment. Just because someone is sad because of loss doesn't mean that's the correct response according to Stoicism. A person who doesn't subscribe to Stoic thought doesn't distinguish what is and what is not within their control. Our job is not to preach our values. Our job is to execute our values in our own minds.

Otherwise, we risk becoming patronizing or showing disdain for someone's feelings. That is not a noble thing to do. We should never waive away someone's pain and say stuff like, "Why are you upset about that? It's not even real!" Well, it might not be real to you. But you are not the other. This means that a Stoic respects other people's emotions. After all, how can someone else tell us what to feel?

When we decide to change our view of the world, it's an internal decision. You could never start living like a Stoic unless you truly believe it's the right approach.

When you're confronted with other people's emotions, you might have the urge to suggest possible solutions. You see someone struggling, and you've seen how a small mindset shift has improved your life—and you want the same for others! I think that's a kind thing to desire. But it can come across as controlling or patronizing.

Stoics believe in the personal power of themselves and others. They didn't think they were any better than other people. And they didn't want to show disdain because they knew others don't appreciate that.

Everyone likes to be their own person. This is actually a good thing. It means you can let others be.

That's how you protect your mood: By not feeling responsible for how others feel. Focus on yourself and be the best person you can be. And if others need your help, you can be there for them.

LETTER 3:
ON MOTIVATING YOURSELF

Every time I lose my motivation or energy, I do the same thing. I return to the pursuit of knowledge. A few weeks ago, I felt a bit unmotivated. You know, it was one of those unexplainable periods that you're just not that excited about things. Usually, I wake up and I'm excited to get to work or to exercise. It was none of that. Nothing bad really happened, and I felt pretty good physically. I just didn't feel like doing much.

Everyone goes through these phases. But many of us get stuck in these phases, and that's risky. No one likes to be in a perpetual state of "I don't feel like doing much" mind. So what can you do to get motivated again?

Try this: When you're lost, unfocused, or lacking motivation, grab a book about a topic you're interested in.

Simply browse the web for anything that you're curious about and that you want to learn more about. It could be anything. Want to become a better writer? Try reading William Zinsser. Want to become a better stock market trader? Check out Jack Schwager's books. Want to learn more about human history? Pick up *The Dawn of Everything* by David Graeber and David Wengrow, which is what I did. I love reading about mankind because the more we understand our ancestors, the more we learn about ourselves. That book by Graeber and Wengrow is really fascinating and provides a new look at human history.

David Graeber, who passed away a month after he finished The Dawn of Everything in 2020, was a very curious person. I had the pleasure to talk to him on my podcast, and I could really feel his excitement about the topics he talked about as an anthropologist. His energy and curiosity were contagious. It inspired me to keep pursuing knowledge no matter what happened in life. Around seven years ago, I decided that I was done with pointless entertainment and boredom. After years of going aimlessly through life, I just had enough of having no direction in life.

Too often, people assume you need some kind of higher aim in life to be functional. If we're not like people who work on specific larger-than-life goals, we think our life is useless. That's not true.

If you don't have a higher purpose, you can make the pursuit of knowledge your purpose. This is also what the

Stoics talked about. Seneca was a critic of the aimless life. He once said: "So I would criticize those who busy themselves on something pointless, but admire those who strive for honorable achievement, the more they put effort into it and do not allow themselves to be overcome and bewitched: I will salute them: 'All the better: rise and breathe deeply and conquer that slope with one breath if you can.' Effort nourishes noble spirits."

When you make an effort to acquire knowledge, you nourish your spirit. Learning gives you energy, even if you don't use every single thing you learn.

While I'm a big believer in applying knowledge, you never know when you will apply what you've learned. For example, I read about investing a lot because I never know when I actually will need a piece of advice. But if I invest the time today to learn, I can refer to that knowledge at some point in the future. And that moment might really change my life. If I never read that wisdom, I could never apply it. When it comes to investing, having knowledge about the history of finance and the stock market helps me to put things in perspective.

Ultimately, whether you use knowledge or not, it's a great way of living. One that gives you energy and can change your life. Seneca said it best: "So what is good? The knowledge of life. What is bad? Ignorance of life." To have knowledge of life, pursue wisdom in books, articles, and through conversations with other people who are on the same path.

When you keep learning, you will never be unmotivated for longer than a few days. Because as soon as you pick up a book that you love, the excitement is so high that the sense of awe propels you forward. Remember: When you're stuck, always return to the pursuit of knowledge.

LETTER 4:
ON DEALING WITH ANXIETY

There are a lot of reasons to be anxious. Not just now, but at any given time in history. It's the human condition. The truth is that we're fragile beings. I can go outside right now for a walk, slip on a banana, hit my head on the curb, and it's lights out. There are a million bad things that could happen to you and me.

As Epictetus once said, "If you want to make progress, stop feeling anxious about things."

It's really difficult to live a happy and peaceful life if you feel anxious all the time. I think it helps if we accept that a little bit of anxiety is a normal part of life. It's just like feeling hungry. When you don't eat for a longer period, your body starts giving you signals. "Hey, you! I'm hungry. Feed me. NOW!" So you grab something to eat and your body stops the signaling. That's actually useful.

But your mind works in the same way—which isn't always helpful. When the mind identifies something it doesn't like, it says, "You better do something about this thing I don't like!" One thing that I used to get anxious about is whether people liked me or not. Can you relate to this? I often thought things like, "What if this person I work with doesn't like me? Why didn't they respond to my email within an hour? Maybe it's because I was in a hurry last time we talked?" So what? You can't make people like you—and that's fine. The world is a big place.

There are always people who will like you. If you're a good person and are aware of your own behavior, there's no need to ever worry about what others think of you. That's not your problem.

What about the economy and the future? Yes, that's another favorite topic for everyone who struggles with anxiety. What if you lose your job? What if there's a new virus? What if people no longer buy your products? We can train ourselves not to be anxious about these things. The key is to practice detachment. Start with small things. Let's say you bought $1000 worth of Bitcoin and the next day, you've lost 10 per cent, which is a very likely outcome. Say to yourself, "I took a risk, and I'm happy to part ways with the $100 I lost. It might come back, or it might not. Either way, I'm happy to detach from this loss so I can have peace of mind. There are more important things."

You see, anxiety is always about fear. We fear that reality is different than our expectations. But reality doesn't have to match our expectations for us to feel less anxious.

Epictetus explained this well: "Things may not work out the way you want. When you choose not to be anxious, you do it in spite of your unfulfilled expectations. What you lose is what you pay for your peace of mind."

You want and expect people to like you, but if that doesn't happen, you should accept it, and move on. Don't give anxiety power over you. Be prepared to pay the price of not being liked. Is that so bad? Is your peace of mind not more important than what your co-workers or strangers think of you?

Build up this mindset slowly and have some patience. It took me a few years to get over my anxiety about the future. But there will always remain some traces. To be honest, anxiety will never fully get out of your system. It's human nature. But with practice, you can make sure anxiety doesn't have a hold over you.

At some point, you will accept that life is what it is.

Some people like you, some don't. Jobs disappear, while new ones are created. Nothing is forever. And for what it's worth, we're not getting out of this thing alive either! There's only one conclusion to this whole story: Nothing is worth giving up your peace of mind for.

LETTER 5:
ON PROTECTING YOURSELF FROM DISAPPOINTMENT

We often try really hard to get what we want and avoid what we don't want. On the one hand, we desire certain things that are related to pleasure. You know, the usual stuff: A good job, more fun experiences, laughter, going to nice restaurants, buying clothes or gadgets, getting a new car, posting funny memes on social media. No one can deny those things are pretty fun. And on the other hand, we try hard to avoid bad things in life.

You also know what that means: Sickness, joblessness, sadness, pain, suffering, hard work, boredom. If it were up to us, our whole life would be one big party! Epictetus, the Stoic philosopher who was born into slavery during Nero's reign and became free after the vicious emperor died, often talked about the foolishness of our expectations. He once said:

"You are being foolish if you expect your children, spouse, or friends to live forever. You don't have the power to make this happen. It is equally naïve to expect everyone will be honest. It is not under your control but in the control of others who may act honestly or dishonestly. Therefore, we are at the mercy of whoever has control over things we desire or detest. You can, however, avoid disappointment and be free if you do not desire or avoid things that other people control."

Ouch. Takes a few moments to process that, right? Epictetus was the most direct (and sometimes blunt) Stoic. I think that's what makes him so credible. When he says things like that, I listen. He's absolutely right when it comes to avoiding disappointment. I created a book proposal for my next book which is about applying the philosophy of Stoicism to wealth building. I self-published my previous books, which meant I didn't have to rely on others for distribution. But it also comes with downsides. When you work with a publisher, you can create a much better piece of work, especially if you work with a great editor. That's also the reason I pursued traditional publishing for my next book, which will be my most important one.

But when you go through a process like that, where there's a lot you don't control, you can get disappointed when you don't get what you want. The whole process took almost a year, from finding the right agent, creating a great proposal, sending it out to publishers, talking to them, and listening to their offers. And at every step, things can go south. When the proposal went out, I received many rejections as well.

To avoid disappointment, I kept focusing on what I control: My actions and belief in the book.

That helped me to stay positive and have great conversations with interested publishers. From Epictetus, I learned to not desire things others control. I didn't desire to get a yes from any publisher. I also didn't desire a specific advance. In fact, I didn't desire to get a deal. I was good with any outcome. If I didn't get an offer or an offer I didn't like, I would've been good with that. It was not something I wanted to avoid. That helped me to stay calm and rational throughout the process. Eventually, several publishers were interested enough to make an offer, and I went with Portfolio/ Penguin because it was really the best fit. The truth is I had a whole plan laid out in case the traditional route didn't pan out.

I knew I couldn't afford to get disappointed. And the best way to avoid that is to always focus on what you control. As Epictetus said, it's foolish to expect we have the power to make certain things happen. That doesn't mean we have to disconnect ourselves from our emotions. We will still be sad when a loved one passes away, even when we realize no one is immortal. That's not the point of Stoicism. The point is to remind yourself of the outcomes as you're going through life.

For example, when you remind yourself that your mother or father will not live forever, you're less likely to go hard on them at the family dinner when you talk about politics.

You think, "It's not worth it to get angry. Soon we will not be here anymore."

Ultimately, Stoicism challenges us to think about the long-term impact of our actions. If we do things we will later regret, we only create inner turmoil.

If we do things that are in line with Stoic beliefs, we avoid regret. As a result, we have inner peace.

LETTER 6:
ON THE CURE FOR FEAR

In one of Seneca's letters to his friend, Lucillius, he shared a lesson he learned about fear: "Cease to hope ... and you will cease to fear."

Isn't hope what propels us forward? Isn't it nihilistic to give up hope? I must be honest; I do think that hope serves a purpose. As the Dalai Lama said: "I find hope in the darkest of days, and focus in the brightest." The topic of hope is a popular one when it comes to motivational posters or social media posts.

And there's truth in what people say about hope. We need to have some kind of faith that tomorrow will be better. Hope can inspire us to be optimistic. But what do you do when tomorrow isn't better? How do you respond when the things you hoped for never come true? We hope for a lot of things...

- "I hope there won't be another Covid surge."
- "I hope I can go on a vacation."
- "I hope she likes me."
- "I hope I get hired."

Let's face it, the majority of the things we hope for will not come true. That's the type of hope Seneca was talking about. He continued: "Fear keeps pace with hope ... both belong to a mind in suspense, to a mind in a state of anxiety through looking into the future. Both are mainly due to projecting our thoughts far ahead of us instead of adapting ourselves to the present."

This couldn't be put in a better way. Hope and fear are the same things. When you experience fear, you hope that something doesn't happen. In the most primitive and ancient way, it's, "I hope this tiger won't eat me!"

But in today's safer world, it's more like, "I hope that the things I don't want will not happen." Think about how often you use the phrase, "I hope" so and so happens. I catch myself saying it casually pretty often. But on a deeper level, I don't hope for things to happen. I do have the faith/hope/belief in a better future. But I have a very abstract type of hope.

I don't want to have a specific type of hope because it only causes fear. When you hope for something, you wish to have the things you want. This is not a peaceful way to live.

Just have faith in the future, and then forget about it! Avoid looking into the future for too long. When you notice that you strongly want things to happen, become aware of your thoughts. Correct your self-talk. This is really important because the way you talk enforces your beliefs.

When you say, "I hope" all the time, you think it's normal behavior. You'll keep hoping, and you'll probably hope for more. And when things don't work out, you become disappointed. I picked up a great technique for avoiding that from Susan Jeffers, the author of *Feel The Fear And Do It Anyway*. In her book, she recommends everyone start "wondering" instead of "hoping."

- Instead of saying: "I hope I get a new job."
- Say: "I wonder what my new job will be."

I like this mindset shift because it's more like how life really is: Unpredictable. When we hope for things, we think we can control life. We think as long as we really want something badly, it will come true. It's a form of feeling in control. I can imagine that many people spend their entire lives hoping for one thing after the other. It's a good way to keep yourself busy.

But if you instead start looking at life as a journey that could lead you anywhere, you go about everything differently. You'll say, "Let's see what happens." And as a Stoic, whatever happens, is fine. So life will be fine.

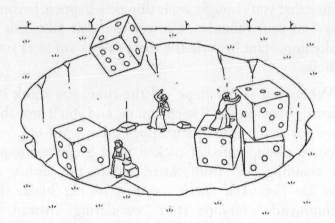

LETTER 7:
ON GIVING YOURSELF A BREAK

Last night, my washing machine broke down. I wanted to quickly wash a sweater that I've been wearing a lot so I could let it dry overnight. At least, that's what I thought when I turned the thing on at 10 p.m. It was supposed to be a quick 60-minute program. When I went to check how many minutes were left on the machine almost an hour later, I saw an error code on the screen. "You better not break down on me!" I said out loud as if the machine could hear me. I knew it, the thing didn't work. I opened the door, and my sweater was drenched in water. I could feel my anger stirring inside.

First, I took the sweater to my bathtub and started centrifuging the thing with my hands, like a cowboy in an old Western washing his shirt in the river. As I was wringing the sweater, I was surprised by how heavy it was on my forearms. I actually thought, "This is a good workout," and felt pretty good about it for a moment.

But after doing it for a while, and realizing it takes a long time to get the water out of the cotton, I started getting annoyed. "Why does this happen right now? Why not during the day?"

I squeezed enough so the sweater didn't drip water anymore and hung it to dry. Then I went back to the washing machine and in my stubbornness, set out to find the problem. I wanted to fix the damn machine right there, right then and started pulling it apart. By the time I was finished, it was midnight, I was sweating profusely, and I was pumped up from the adrenaline caused by my anger. This whole episode was totally trivial. Stuff like this happens all the time. We all experience anger in some shape or form. For me, it often comes when things don't do what they are supposed to, like my washing machine that doesn't want to wash. In the end, the problem was fixed, but at what cost?

Seneca explained the importance of managing anger: "Anger, if not restrained, is frequently more hurtful to us than the injury that provokes it." This isn't just emotionally true; there are physical implications too.

When you're angry or when you beat yourself up because you're so critical of yourself (which is a form of anger towards yourself), you release cortisol. This isn't only bad for your body, it's also bad for your sleep. Cortisol is the primary stress hormone of the human body, and it increases sugars in the bloodstream so your brain operates better during life-and death situations.

It's a great biological process that likely once saved us from saber-toothed tigers, but it also has the power to destroy us when we get stressed about meaningless things. Cortisol slows down your metabolism, which can seriously disrupt your digestive system. 2000 years ago, Seneca probably didn't know about the science of cortisol, but he could feel the negative impact anger and stress had.

Let's be real: Every time you get angry, you're only harming yourself. The things that make you angry are often less hurtful than the effect of anger on your body.

That doesn't mean you should never get angry. Go ahead and get angry when someone threatens your livelihood. But don't get angry with yourself when something goes wrong, or when you do something wrong in your own eyes. So many of us treat ourselves with anger, that we can use more self-love. Go easy on yourself.

After the whole washing machine episode, I had to laugh because it was so stupid. I stood there sweaty, at 12 a.m., fixing a washing machine, while I should've been in bed. I also thought, "At least this experience wasn't meaningless because I can write about it." The better response would be to laugh right at the moment I found a drenched sweater in the washing machine, but you know what they say: Better late than never.

Instead of beating yourself up and being your own antagonist, be your own comedian.

Observe your behavior, and instead of getting angry, become aware of the shortness of life. Realize that most things are not worth getting angry over and laugh it off. Life will be better that way.

MANAGING YOUR THOUGHTS

"The chief task in life is simply this: to identify and separate matters so that I can say clearly to myself which are externals not under my control, and which have to do with the choices I actually control."

— Epictetus

LETTER 8:
ON CHANGING YOUR MINDSET—
NOT YOUR SURROUNDINGS

I've been feeling more and more frustrated with my surroundings lately. Every day starts to blend together. You wake up in the same bed, look at the same view, eat your breakfast in the same room, see the same neighbors, and so forth. This is the force that drives so many of us to travel. This feeling of getting bored, frustrated, and annoyed with your life is completely normal. I feel that a few times a year as well.

Here's how I deal with that to make it go away quickly. This desire to change your surroundings is not new. The Stoics wrote about it a lot. Seneca said it best when his friend, Lucilius, complained about how boring his life was, which made Lucilius feel depressed: "Do you think you are the only man this happened to and feel amazed as if this was a new experience, that after such prolonged travels and with such changes of scene you have not shaken off your sadness and depression? You should change your attitude, not your surroundings." He's right. Why are we surprised that we get down?

I find it especially weird that we insist on blaming our surroundings. "I just need to get out of here." As if a change of scenery will make our problems go away.

There's no such thing. We think that the problem lies in our surroundings—but the problem is actually our mindset. The problem is not you. It's human nature to get used to your surroundings. I haven't met a single person who doesn't get depressed by their life if there's no novelty. It doesn't matter how great your life is, at some point, you adapt your standards. And when that happens, we feel depressed like Lucilius. Sometimes you meet these overly optimistic people who always pretend everything is great. You ask, "How are you?" And they say, "Wonderful!" Those are the worst cases. Who on earth feels "wonderful" all the time?! Give me a break. Life is hard and anyone who pretends it's always amazing is fooling themselves.

But here's the thing: You *can* snap out of your gloomy mindset. There's nothing wrong with you; the entity, soul, consciousness, or whatever you want to call yourself. I know this sounds esoteric, but here's what I remind myself of every time I realize I'm blaming my surroundings: The solution is not out there. The solution is right where you are. All you need to do is change the way you look at things.

Don't immediately try to change other things—even if you have control over them. "But that's what the Stoics say you should do! Focus on what you control. And I have control over my decisions. And I decide to get a new job or move to another city!" That's correct. But Stoicism is more subtle and complex than most people think. Just because you control certain things, it doesn't mean you have to exert your control. The key is to operate from a place of equanimity. Be calm and neutral. Let that be your standard method of operation. Make your decisions from there.

When it comes to changing your surroundings, I look at it this way: I would love to take a trip to the Caribbean and do some snorkeling. But I don't need anything. I'm good the way that I am. Will I go when the time is right? Probably. Will I stay put and enjoy my days if it's a hassle to go? 100 per cent. There's no need to change anything to find inner peace. It's right there where you are. You just have to change your mindset to see it.

LETTER 9:
ON OBSERVING YOUR MIND

Marcus Aurelius' *Meditations* was never meant to be published as a book. It's a collection of notes, scribbles, and musings he wrote for himself. One of those notes to himself is this: "My mind. What is it? What am I making of it? What am I using it for?" Throughout *Meditations*, you often see Aurelius asking himself questions. I like this way of thinking because he's not making any statements or assumptions. Instead of assuming how the mind works, he asks a question. What is the mind? What am I using it for? If you know how you think, you can make much better use of your mind.

While it's hard to answer the first question (no one knows exactly what the mind is), you can think about what you're using your mind for. For example, some days I notice that I'm lost in thought from the moment I wake up. Instead of getting out of bed and starting my day, I have no focus at all. That still happens occasionally. But before I started practicing Stoicism, I would often think about things I had no control over. I often had anxiety about the future. What if my business fails? What if I have to get a job I hate? What if my relationship fails? What if <fill in the blanks>.

I've learned to stop worrying and to focus on the present more. But I don't control my consciousness, and sometimes I think a lot about my work, writing, goals, future plans, etc. I think about the books I would like to write, the events I want to organize, the places I want to visit, you know, the standard daydreaming type thoughts. But when you get lost in those thoughts, you also tend to listen to your thoughts.

The other day, I thought, "I want to organize an event for people who are interested in philosophy and personal growth." It sounds great, but it's not something I really want to do right now. It just sounded nice in my head. To bring it back to the question Marcus Aurelius posed to himself: What am I using my mind for? In that case, I was using my mind to daydream and entertain myself with interesting fantasies. Having ideas is great, but do you really need to spend so much time playing out scenarios in your mind? It's just like replaying conversations in your mind after they took place. Do you do that as well? Isn't that a big waste of time?

> **Nothing will change if you keep replaying a conversation in your mind. You can go over everything and change what you said in your mind, but you can't go back in time to actually have the same conversation again.**

This is another way of being lost in mind. And it's the perfect example of having useless thoughts. Sure, it's useful to think about lessons you've learned from certain events, but it's not useful to replay past events in your mind like a broken record.

To avoid wasting your time and energy on useless thoughts, you can observe your mind more. Simply grab a notebook and start journaling like Marcus Aurelius. The key is to journal around a particular challenge or question. For example, when I wanted to improve my skills as a stock trader, I asked myself, "What happens when I make mistakes with trading?"

Through journaling, I noticed that I would often give in to my emotions like greed and the need to be right. One thing I did a lot in the past was "averaging down." Let's say you're a momentum trader (not a long-term investor), you only want to buy stocks that go up. So when you buy a stock at 50, you buy it because you think it keeps going up. And you keep adding as it moves higher. A disciplined momentum trader never adds to their position at 49. That's averaging down. But I would do that because I thought, "If I buy more at a lower price, my potential profit would be even more!" That was my greed speaking. And I've had a few occasions I kept adding to a position as it was going ten to twenty percent lower. That was because I had to prove I was right: "This stock WILL go up eventually. I'm just going to buy more as it goes lower. It's just a matter of time!"

Through journaling, I noticed I was listening to those types of unhelpful thoughts. By applying Stoic principles to my trading strategy, and by noticing my greed and need to be right at the moment, I stopped it.

I haven't averaged down in a long time. Journaling about your thoughts is really simple. There's no right or wrong way to do it. You simply write down everything that pops up in your head. But always start with a question. And then simply observe your mind on paper. The more you observe, the more you can spot unhelpful behavior. All you need to do now is do less of the unhelpful things and focus on doing things that help you to be a balanced person.

LETTER 10:
ON GUARDING YOUR MIND

In the first letter, I talked about useless information. But what does that mean? To me, anything that doesn't have a positive impact on my life is useless. That's why I love reading books instead of scrolling through social media. Most stuff on social media is like sugar. It might give you a quick high, but it doesn't have a positive impact on your life overall. But that's not the only type of useless information. It's everywhere.

For example, I love watching the NBA. But I avoid consuming all kinds of information around the league. Who cares what some ESPN analyst wrote about how LeBron James played last night? Consuming that information is not a good use of time. I'd rather watch the actual game, go on a walk, read a book, have a conversation with a friend, etc.

Everyone has an opinion about everything.
But instead of listening to everyone,
we need to listen more to ourselves.

We can learn more about that from the legendary stock trader, Jesse Livermore. He was successful on Wall Street in the two decades before the Great Depression—and he made a lot of big trades that put him on the radar of anyone interested in the market. But at some point, he retreated from the Street. He just didn't want to have anything to do with people who asked him for stock tips or influenced his thinking. He wanted to rely on his own judgment. He once said: "I never wanted to be part of a group of stock market traders, especially those traders who gathered in the brokerage office. My main reason was that I needed continuity of thought. I needed to be able to have more than 15 minutes of uninterrupted thought."

I can't stress how important this is for your quality of thinking. One of the best things I've done for my career is to retreat from the publishing world. I prefer not to mingle with other writers. It's nothing personal. Being part of a group influences your thinking. Eventually, every member of the group will have the same types of thoughts and opinions. Rely on your own observation and judgment. Don't allow another person to form an opinion for you. There's another reason why I guard my mind.

When you consume information, it will impact your mood—whether you like it or not. No one has enough mental power to resist outside influence.

We can only limit it. There's this concept called Affect Heuristic. It basically says that if you're in a fearful mindset, you'll make fearful decisions. You can replace "fearful" with any type of emotion. Let's say social media makes you feel unworthy. Do you really want to go through your day making decisions feeling that way? Of course not. So get rid of information that makes you feel bad, anxious, weak, jealous, or simply has no use.

I used to be friends with this guy who was a huge Boston Celtics fan. The guy listened to all the podcasts, watched all the talk shows, pre-game shows, half-time reports, and postgame analyses. He knew everything about all the players on the Celtics roster. On top of that, he also knew everything about their personal lives and history. "You see that guy?! His sister is a chiropractor." Wait, what? I can't think of a single reason why you need to know that. His favorite team won't play any better if he knows everything about them.

Isn't it better to spend all of those hours we dedicate to pointless consumption on improving our relationships? Instead of sitting on the couch with your eyes glued to your phone, have a conversation with your partner, or call your friend. Anything that's actually useful or good!

Ultimately, this all comes down to using our time in the best way possible. We all know that our time and energy are limited. So we need to be selective about how we spend it.

Next time you're about to consume something, ask yourself, "Is this worth spending my time on?"

The goal is to be more conscious about the information you allow in your brain. It doesn't matter whether it's a news article or a tweet; only consume things that have a positive impact on your life.

LETTER 11:
ON NOT GETTING DISTRACTED

I've been in Fuengirola, a town in the south of Spain, for the past month. I came here with my brother and my mother to enjoy the weather and explore the area. I've also kept writing. Last week, my family went back home, and I decided to focus on writing my book. I could go out, explore, and connect with some locals. But I decided to stay focused and make progress.

I love to write and I see this as my purpose. I live for this. And I'm committed to writing the best book I possibly can. The book is about how you can apply Stoicism to wealth building. It's something I've been doing since 2015, and it's worked out well.

One big idea that has inspired me to be so focused on what I do is something Marcus Aurelius said: "No random actions, none not based on underlying principles."

To me, that means everything you do has a reason. But not just any type of reason. If you follow a certain philosophy or religion, your actions are based on the underlying principles of what you believe in. I happen to live by Stoic principles, which are straightforward:

- Focus on what you control
- Live in agreement with nature

There are other principles, but they always lead back to those two things. The first part is straightforward. When you focus on what you control, you get clarity. You'll soon enough figure out that you control very little in life. So you can concentrate on spending your energy on those things (particularly on being the best version of yourself). The second principle, living in agreement with nature might sound less clear. To the Stoics, humans are rational beings who also should behave rationally. To live well is to live in harmony with the facts of life. And one fact of life is that we quickly get distracted. I experienced that the first week I got here. There's so much to do around here, and the weather is so great that I can fill up my days with leisure.

Living a good life is about not getting distracted.

Think about the times you were feeling at your best. What types of moments were that? I bet it was when you were fully engaged. Whether it was an experience with your friend or partner, or it was working on a project you were passionate about.

The moment we lose our focus and wander aimlessly, we get frustrated. That's why I believe every person should have some kind of personal passion project. Something you work on for fun and pleasure. Something that you fully control. No matter what's going on in the world, you can always work on your project. Writing does that for me because it's a solo pursuit. But it could be anything that is truly yours. It could be any form of art. But it could also be a fitness or health project. One of my friends who's turning 40 in two years set a goal for himself: 40 with a six-pack.

Today, he ran a half marathon in 1:35 hours. And the average time is around 2 hours. He clocked a time that only advanced runners get. Pretty impressive. And he's running faster than when he was in his twenties. Why? He has an aim. His training is no longer random. As Marcus Aurelius said, no random actions. When it comes to his health, he does everything to be his fittest self today and keeps it up when he gets 40. And after that, he'll probably come up with another project or aim.

We all need these higher goals, projects, and ambitions to live our life a certain way. If you have a reason to do things, you wake up with clarity.

You get after the things you set out to achieve. And when you always focus on goals that lie within your control, you are the determining factor, not other people or luck.

LETTER 12:
ON THE VALUE OF
SINGLE-MINDED FOCUS

What's something you are currently working towards? Maybe you want to get into a top university, apply for a job at the best company in your field, or become the best expert in your area of expertise.

We achieve good things when we do great work. And to do great work, we need to focus. As Seneca once said: "To be everywhere is to be nowhere."

If you want to achieve anything, you need to focus on that one thing. When your focus and energy are all over the place, you never make any meaningful progress. This idea sounds so simple, and yet it's one of the hardest things to do in life. I can't tell you how often I work on improving my focus. It's an endless challenge because our focus fluctuates all the time.

Here are a few things that influence your ability to focus on what's important to you.

Mental health: When you're feeling down, you're often more inclined to have distracting thoughts. You do everything to distract your thoughts from the thing you actually want to achieve. It seems like your mind is working against you.

Secondary activities: Primary activities are those truly important things in life like taking care of yourself, spending time with your loved ones, getting enough rest, and making meaningful progress in your career. Everything else is secondary: Social media, entertainment, gossip, online dating, gambling, playing games, and so forth. When you spend more time on secondary activities than primary ones, you're lacking focus.

Lack of a big goal: When you don't have a big goal in life, you won't have anything meaningful to work on. You feel like you're not making progress. If you work towards a big goal, something that takes years to accomplish, you have clarity and focus.

When you take care of your mental health, work on primary activities, and have a big goal, you can make A LOT of progress in stepping up your level of focus. Sometimes, it's best to have single-minded focus for a set amount of time. For example, during the last month, I spent about 90 per cent of my time, energy, and mental bandwidth completing my new book. Within that single month, I finished the first draft. I wrote more in one month than in the six prior months.

That's the power of single-minded focus. By eliminating most things from your life for some time, you can make so much progress. This is something the former Navy Seal and ultramarathon runner David Goggins talks about often. His ambition is to be the best among the best. To achieve that, you can't be balanced sometimes, as he writes:

"If you truly want to become uncommon amongst the uncommon, it will require sustaining greatness for a long period of time. It requires staying in constant pursuit and putting out unending effort. This may sound appealing but will require everything you have to give and then some. Believe me, this is not for everyone because it will demand singular focus and may upset the balance in your life." I've never met a person who was the best at their job, competed in sports events, and had a highly active social life. We can't underestimate the time and energy it takes to be great at anything; whether you want to be the greatest parent you can be or the best athlete, you can't be everything at the same time. Something's got to give. If you try to do everything, you either burn out or break something. You might blow up your work or your relationships. As the saying goes: You can have it all, but not all at the same time.

Look, I do love to live a balanced life. But the key is that I only balance a few things. I've decided that I'm all-in on work, exercise, and family. And occasionally I have to get even more focused, like the month I really went deep into finishing my book. I don't mind not having a rich social life. I'd rather balance the things I focus on.

This is what Goggins means when he says that trying to be great may upset the balance in your life. It sure will if you try to spend your time and energy on too many things. You have to make choices.

You're better off, mentally and professionally, by being really focused on the things that matter to you.

And sometimes, you can even step that up as I did with my book. But that's not something I recommend doing for a long time because you'll end up overworked. We still need our rest and downtime.

LETTER 13:
ON HAVING A HEALTHY MIND

In The Netherlands, where I grew up, the phrase common sense means "gezond verstand." The literal translation to English is "healthy mind." I've always liked that translation better than common sense for some reason. When I was reading Marcus Aurelius' *Meditations* for the first time, I also noticed that he talked about the concept of having a healthy mind. He wrote:

"A healthy pair of eyes should see everything that can be seen and not say, "No! Too bright!" (which is a symptom of ophthalmia). A healthy sense of hearing or smell should be prepared for any sound or scent; a healthy stomach should have the same reaction to all foods, as a mill to what it grinds. So too a healthy mind should be prepared for anything."

That makes you think: What's a healthy mind? Let's start with the reverse. What's an unhealthy mind? To think about this, we need to let go of the idea of common sense. For example, a person could have sound judgment and be a logical thinker, but still have an unhealthy mind. Here's what an unhealthy mind means to me. A mind that's…

- Worried; constantly thinking about things outside its control

- Inconsistent; feeling happy one day and sad the next for no reason

- Unfocused; not able to concentrate on important things

- Insecure; not satisfied with itself

When you flip these things, you have a healthy mind. Can we all have a 100 per cent healthy mind all of the time? Well, I think that's something an unhealthy mind would ask. Think about it.

A healthy mind is the opposite of worried—it's peaceful. It doesn't care about the things that are either outside its control or are unrealistic.

The nature of human beings is that we make mistakes. We can't live a perfect life. It's not important whether we make mistakes or not. It's important that we hold our composure and don't lose our cool.

Aurelius said that an unhealthy mind is one that "keeps saying, "Are my children all right?" or "Everyone must approve of me." These are just two examples of unhealthy thinking. I think most of us know what really healthy behavior is. No one is surprised when you say,

"It's not healthy if you're happy one day and sad the next." We know that's not normal. But we often don't know what normal looks like.

It's actually a good question. What's normal behavior? When you grow up in a family that always complains and argues about almost everything (like me), you think it's normal to live that way. Since I grew up that way, I thought it was normal to argue a lot when you're in a relationship. It wasn't until I was 30 that I learned that's not healthy. Sometimes we're just not aware of what's healthy. That's why I like philosophy so much. Because it's about finding the answers to living a good, and healthy, life.

It's an ongoing process of trying to become better. And having a healthy mind is one of those things we should always strive for.

KNOWING YOURSELF BETTER

**"What progress, you ask, have I made? I have begun
to be a friend to myself."**

— Hecato of Rhodes

LETTER 14:
ON KNOWING THYSELF
(AND ACTING ACCORDINGLY)

Years ago, I bought an SUV. I convinced myself that I needed a big car so I could go on more trips and that a big car would come in handy when I had to move house. I spent twenty grand to buy an SUV (a lot of money for me at the time) and just used it in the exact same way as my previous car. I didn't go on more trips, and I didn't move around a bunch of stuff. I just spent more on gas and insurance. That's because I don't really like to do those things anyway. I just liked the idea of those activities.

One of the most important ideas of Western philosophy is the concept of knowing yourself. "To know thyself is the beginning of wisdom," as Socrates famously said. It's good advice. But how do you actually apply it in daily life?

By the looks of it, most people don't apply the idea of "knowing thyself" to their decisions. The funny thing is that we often force ourselves to do things we're unsuited for. For example, I've always been an introvert. And I generally don't like strangers or being in large crowds. It's just not my thing. I don't like small talk with vague acquaintances. But for many years, I tried being more sociable. I went to parties, conferences, social events, concerts, clubs, you name it. And everywhere I went, I ended up just spending time with a handful of people I knew anyway.

I think we all know ourselves—how can we not? After all, you can only be yourself. From the moment you wake up until you go to bed, you're right there with your thoughts and personality. The problem is that most of us lack the confidence to actually live in agreement with who we are. It's not easy to do that. Sometimes you need to push yourself to be yourself.

Isn't that a tragedy? We know who we are, but for whatever reason—fear, social pressure, insecurity—we don't live based on our self-knowledge. That's how we often end up in bad situations. We take jobs that are not a fit for who we are. We start relationships with people who we're not compatible with. And so forth. Stoic philosophy stresses deliberate action. In Epictetus' Discourses, there's a section where he talks about how one should think things through:

"In each action that you undertake, consider what comes before and what follows after, and only then proceed to the action itself. Otherwise, you'll set about it with enthusiasm because you've never given any thought to the consequences that will follow, and then you'll give up in an ignominious fashion when one or another of them makes its appearance."

How often have you set about something with enthusiasm, only to find out later that it actually wasn't for you? I've read about how a lot of people rushed to move out of cities during the first year of Covid. Sure, it sounds nice: the idea of moving from a metropolitan area to someplace quieter. You'll escape the traffic, annoying people, high taxes, lofty house prices, and so forth. But if you love city life, you won't enjoy the suburbs of smaller towns in Arizona or Florida. That's why a lot of people regret their move and have wanted to move back.

Look, we can never fully avoid undesirable situations. And sometimes you just have to try something before you know if you like it or not. But there's definitely a lot of hurt, sadness, and pain we can avoid. We can also avoid wasting our time and money. When we're honest about who we are and the lifestyle we enjoy, we no longer feel the pressure to do certain things. We think before we act. And it's really not that hard.

Whenever you need to make a big decision, try to ask yourself: What are the ultimate outcomes I'm looking for? Does this align with who I actually am? What I'm actually good at? What do I actually enjoy? Will this help me reach my ultimate goals? As Epictetus said, think about the consequences: Good and bad. If that's in line with who you are, then go for it. If it's not, don't.

LETTER 15:
ON YOUR INNER STRENGTH

Throughout 2020, I often thought, "What a wasted year." There's so much we couldn't do because of the pandemic, so many plans we missed out on. Think of the holiday season. Normally, around that time of the year, most of us are out a lot. I'm not a fan of cold weather, but I don't mind going out then. The shops all look festive, Christmas music puts people in a good mood, and coffee tastes so much better after you've been out in the cold for a few hours.

We can still shop and buy coffee in most cities, but it's not the same. By now, three-quarters into the pandemic, most of us had enough. First, there was shock. Then, there was acceptance and making the best of it. Now, there's dread.

During moments of dread, we need to remind ourselves we have the inner strength to keep going.

I know you don't want to get out of bed some days, or maybe want to go back to bed at noon, but you're strong enough to keep moving forward. Epictetus said this beautifully: "Remember that for every challenge you face, you have the resources within you to cope with that challenge. If you are inappropriately attracted to someone, you will find you have the resource of self-restraint. When you have pain, you have the resource of endurance. When you are insulted, you have the resource of patience."

If you think this way, you will find that you have an answer to everything that life throws at you. The problem is that we sometimes forget we're actually strong beings. Think about the people who endured the Holocaust. Viktor Frankl wrote about it in *Man's Search For Meaning*. I love that book. It reminds me that you and I have similar DNA as the people who survived that horror.

Lying in bed with our electric blankets, we think we're becoming soft. But that's not the case. We're simply forgetting that we have the resources of strength within us. It's like going through your basement and finding useful things you didn't even know you had.

The other day I went through my storage and found these great bookends I tucked away when I moved house several years ago. I'd totally forgotten about them. Turns out I can use those in my current condo.

The mental equivalent of going through your storage is reflection. I do this through journaling. It's good to think about the things you've done in the past. Too often, we forget about our own accomplishments and strengths. If you've done something once, who says you can't do it again? If you endured the pandemic during summer, you can endure it during winter. If you've switched careers once, you can do it again. If you've moved to a different city, you can move again.

Remember that you are stronger than you think at any given moment.

We all have these inherent mechanisms that are meant to help us go through life. As Epictetus said, "When you have pain, you have the resource of endurance." It's all inside you. You just need to dust it off and use it again.

LETTER 16:
ON CRAFTING YOUR LIFE STORY

Everybody has a narrative about who they are and what they are capable of. You probably tell yourself all kinds of things without even knowing it. I have a story about myself that I quit as soon as things get a bit hard.

During the first few years when I started my blog and worked towards becoming a professional writer, I would occasionally look at jobs. Especially when things didn't work out. I would launch products in the first year, and if I didn't earn the amount of money I wanted, I would get discouraged. My mind told me, "Just quit. It's too hard. Go and get a job and you'll be safe."

But after looking at some jobs, I realized that if I can tell myself to quit, I can also tell myself to keep going. After all, achieving a worthwhile goal is not easy and requires perseverance. The ancient Stoics were masters at changing the narrative. They looked at every situation in life as an opportunity to adjust the story we tell about ourselves. For example, when something bad happens to us—losing our job, failing to achieve a goal, getting yelled at, being made fun of—we often let it influence our self-image. We let bad things harm our emotions and well-being.

The Stoics believed in personal power. They believed that every person has the ability to give their own meaning to situations.

As Marcus Aurelius famously said about bad things that happen to us: "Choose not to be harmed—and you won't feel harmed. Don't feel harmed—and you haven't been." To anyone who hasn't lived according to Stoic values, this is an alien concept. Society is brought up with the idea that every person has "emotional baggage." We're told that our past influences our present. What happened to us yesterday can scar our personality today. Sometimes it's useful to process what's happened in our past and to try to work through it. But it's also important not to let our stories about ourselves trap us.

Instead, the Stoics believed that you have the power, at any moment, to look differently at anything in life. You cannot change what happens to you. You can change the meaning you give to what happens. For example, when someone at work gives you the feeling you're incompetent, you can say two things:

1. This person is right. I'm no good.

2. This person doesn't know me. I'm doing my best, which is all I can do. I'm good with that.

The former is what causes emotional problems. The latter gives you peace of mind. Whether we like it or not, we all have this narrative about ourselves that continues to evolve over time. And often, it evolves in one direction. If you often talk negatively to yourself, you probably will only do more of that. But if you're objective and not overly positive or overly negative, you'll keep living a balanced life. And if there's one thing we can't get enough of, it's balance.

**Never forget: YOU create your own life story.
YOU have the power to change your attitude
at any given moment.**

Does that mean you can change your entire life in a moment? We all know that's not realistic. But we also know that we can change our attitude because that doesn't require much. Just a belief that it's possible.

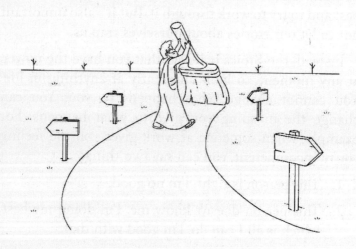

LETTER 17:
ON REMEMBERING YOUR
TRUE SELFWORTH

Every time there's a large-scale marketing event going on around a holiday, like Black Friday or Fourth of July sales, I use it as an opportunity to practice Stoicism. While all these companies are trying to persuade us to buy their products and services, I take the time to strengthen my mind. I learned this from Seneca. He wrote this to Lucilius: "Think that nothing deserves admiration except the mind, which being itself great counts nothing else as great."

The Stoics should see us now! We frequently confuse our selfworth with our possessions. "If I have a valuable watch, it means I'm valuable, right?" Of course not. And you can replace 'watch' with any other external thing. An exclusive car, purse, suit, dress, shoes, TV, sound system, you name it. We use possessions to signal our worth. For a Stoic, that's about as low as you can get. They admired the mind—not one's possessions.

I remember when I bought my first "cool" car. This was back in 2013. I started making some money with our family business, and instead of saving the money, or investing, I decided to buy a car with a V10 diesel engine. It was a VW Touareg that had enough torque to pull a jumbo jet. I drove it with pride. And people gave the car compliments all the time. "Wow, I saw that thing on Top Gear. It can pull a 747, right? That's badass."

My response? "Thank you." As if I'm the car. The truth is that you are not your possessions. When people compliment something we own, we take it personally. We start identifying ourselves with the object. The Stoics were indifferent to possessions and externals because they realized anything that can be given, can be removed. So what does that mean for our daily lives? Your self-worth depends on the things that can't be removed from you. Even the body is fragile, subject to illness and aging. But the mind, that's a different story. As long as it's just functioning, it will not disappoint you.

Seneca says, "Let the man who enters our house admire us rather than our furnishings."

Now, that doesn't mean we should have an empty house and only say to people, "Look at how smart I am!" That's another form of signaling. The Stoics didn't need to impress others with their knowledge or lifestyle. They didn't brag about how virtuous they were. From the outside, they seemed totally intune with society. But internally, they lived like a philosopher.

They practiced thrift—but they also didn't treat it like self-punishment.

Life's too short to take it to the extreme. Just remember that you are not your possessions.

Otherwise, if you lose something that you value, you might feel less complete. You will keep searching for new things to make you whole again. This is the true reason for the rat race. We take jobs we hate so we can buy things we don't actually need.

Does all of this mean we should stay away from buying altogether? Of course not! I always buy supplies in bulk when they are on sale. It's a great way to save money. But I don't spend all day searching for deals. That's how I once ended up wasting four hours and more than four hundred bucks on work-out gear. I didn't use two-thirds of the stuff I bought. That taught me an important lesson. If I need something, I buy that specific thing. But I get on with my day.

You don't need to buy anything today to feel good about yourself. You're not missing out on anything. We all know that Black Friday is just another reason that companies use to get in our wallets. Remember that there are other times of the year when things are on sale as well. Spend today on things that make you a better human.

LETTER 18:
ON STANDING BEHIND YOUR VALUES AT ALL TIMES

Last week I went to a friend's party. It was in a private area of an establishment, and it was a lot of fun. At some point, we were sitting outside with a group when one of the people there pulled out a joint. I don't mind other people's business. But I don't like being close to people who are so addicted they can't be at a normal party without using. If they do it in private or with others who are into that lifestyle, so be it.

I simply left that space because I didn't like the energy of that group. I could sense they were not about personal growth and positivity. So I happily left. When we decide to be a certain person with certain ideals, we can't just throw out our ideals at the first sign of peer pressure or temptation.

As Epictetus once said, we must be the same person in every situation: "Decide first what type of person you want to be and stick to it. Be the same person whether you are by yourself or with others."

This is a liberating way of living. You never have to think about how to behave in certain situations. "How should I behave at work?" Just like you behave at home or in front of your family. If you live by proper values, you have nothing to hide.

I can proudly say that I'm the same person when I'm with family, friends, employees, and most importantly when I write. This is how I think and how I live. If people think that's too intense or serious, so what?

What matters is that *you* like *yourself*. Honestly, if people think you're a certain way, it doesn't matter. If the person at the party thinks I'm not fun, the feeling is mutual. I don't have the urge to be liked by strangers or acquaintances. If I like myself, and the important people in my life like me, that's all I need.

Marcus Aurelius also talked about this idea. In his journal, he wrote that he aspired to always be honest and straightforward. If he truly lived that way, "no one can say truthfully that you are not a straightforward or honest person. That anyone who thinks that believes a falsehood. The responsibility is all yours; no one can stop you from being honest or straightforward. Simply resolve not to go on living if you aren't. It would be contrary to the logos."

Who do you want to be? What type of person would make you proud of yourself? Be that person, always.

As Marcus said, the responsibility is all yours. No one can stop you from being a certain way.

MAKING BETTER DECISIONS

"We must concern ourselves absolutely with the things that are under our control and entrust the things not in our control to the universe."

— Musonius Rufus

LETTER 19:
ON MAKING YOUR OWN DECISIONS

How often do you decide to go a certain direction, whether that's in your career or personal life, and you end up deviating from where you wanted to end up? And how often do you let other people allow your decision-making? For many of us, those two things are interconnected. For example, we want to pursue a creative career, but we let our partner or parents talk us out of it. Instead, we take a job that's considered desirable by others.

Too many of us listen too much to what others say and think. In our endless quest to please the people in our lives, we become the product of what others want.

When I had a corporate job, I had two co-workers, John and Ethan (not their real names), who also wanted to quit and start their own businesses. I wanted to have a career that gave me inner satisfaction but also paid the bills. It's been almost seven years since I quit that job and had conversations with John and Ethan about how amazing it sounded to be your own boss. Not long after that, John also gave his notice and started a consulting firm. Last week, I caught up with Ethan, who has had three different jobs since then.

He can't stand being a worker, but he just can't take the plunge. That's because he was too concerned with other people's opinions. He's one of the most considerate people I know, and he always listens to other people. But as the ancient

Stoic philosopher Epictetus counseled, it's more important to decide something and stick to it. He said:

"Once you undertake to do something, stick with it and treat it as something that should be carried through. Don't pay attention to what people say. It should not influence you in any way."

This is really hard to do in real life because people are often quick to share opinions. Every time I talk about something I plan to do with my family or friends, someone shares their opinion: "I would do this," or, "I would never do something like that." And then they continue talking about what *they* would do. There's nothing wrong with that, and it's a part of social life. We share our opinions freely, even when people don't ask for them. I don't think that's a bad thing. The bad thing is letting other people's opinions stand in the way of your decisions.

When you're still in the decision-making phase, and you're looking for feedback, it's good to have input from others. But let's say you've already made a decision and you share it with someone you love. What usually happens? If you go to bed that night second-guessing yourself, something's not right.

You're letting other people get in your head too much. It's difficult to find a balance between being open to people's advice and being indecisive.

When you want to please everyone in your life, you end up harming your own sense of self-worth. It's a form of suffering.

You don't have to do everything for yourself because that's the recipe for ending up alone. But every person in life must also make their own decisions when it comes to personal matters. This includes things like who you spend time with, what type of work you have, whether you want kids, who you want to have a romantic relationship with, and so forth. You don't need to let others make the decisions for you when you're deciding on things like that.

Decide to live your life as you think is right while keeping your own morals and principles in mind. Decision-making should not lead to suffering, but to lasting inner satisfaction. It's a matter of balance and taking charge at the same time. There's nothing better than deciding to do something, and then actually doing it.

LETTER 20:
ON ADJUSTING YOUR PLANS

What were your plans at the start of this year? I wanted to move to spend a few months in Spain to learn the language and try out new things. I've been to different Spanish cities over the years and I always felt at home. I had gotten pretty far with my plans at the start of 2020. I made sure I had no long-term commitments and was looking at properties. But like the rest of the world, I had to adjust my plans. We were all forced to participate in a classic Stoic exercise. This is something Epictetus talked about in his philosophy school. He said:

"When you are traveling by ship, you can go to the shore, enjoy the scenery, collect shells, or pick flowers. But when you are called back to the ship, you need to drop everything and hurry back, otherwise the ship may leave without you."

That was 2020 in a nutshell. We were somewhere enjoying the scenery, maybe picking some flowers. Some of us were already looking at other places to visit on our ship. But we were called back to the ship abruptly: "We're going home, everybody."

In life, we make up all kinds of plans and goals. But we must be prepared to give up everything when something unexpected happens. Let's be honest, was this pandemic really unexpected? Why do we feel so blindsided by this crisis? It reminds me of the first time I lost someone close to me, my grandmother. She wasn't in good health for the last years of her life. But when she passed, it hit me pretty hard. This was before I practiced Stoicism. In recent years, I've adopted a different mindset about life: We must be able to give up everything when it's called back. We have many things in life that we value; our family, friends, career, business, hobbies, car, investments, you name it. We feel like we have a right to have those relationships or objects.

But in reality, we own nothing, and nothing is owed to us. We're guests who temporarily walk this planet. This mindset shift has helped me. I look at everything in life as borrowed from someone I personally know.

Think about it. How do you act if you borrow something from a friend? You don't get attached, but at the same time, you also take care of it. Live your life like that. Your job, house (even if you bought it), car, assets, and even relationships are not yours. Nothing is truly yours. Crazy, right? But we know on some level that this is true. That doesn't mean we can't have a good time and get close to people. That's a misconception about Stoicism, you know. Some narrow-minded people think it's "dangerous" to live more like the Stoics or to focus more on the self. They don't get it, and that's fine. The truth is that the Stoics cared immensely about their friends and family. They dedicated most of their lives to encouraging others to live well. If that's not altruistic, I don't know what is. When you inspire the people in your life to be happier and more tranquil, all of your lives will be better.

"Does all of this mean we can't plan or set goals? If everything is borrowed, what's the point?"

Plan all you want! Enjoy your friendships, career, and even material possessions. I'm all about that. I love to plan everything. Just don't get attached to your plans. Always be flexible. As our friend Epictetus said, be ready when the ship departs. As you're creating plans for the holidays and the new year, keep that in the back of your mind. If something falls through, quickly let go of your old plan, and come up with something new. Think creatively and never stop trying to make the best of it.

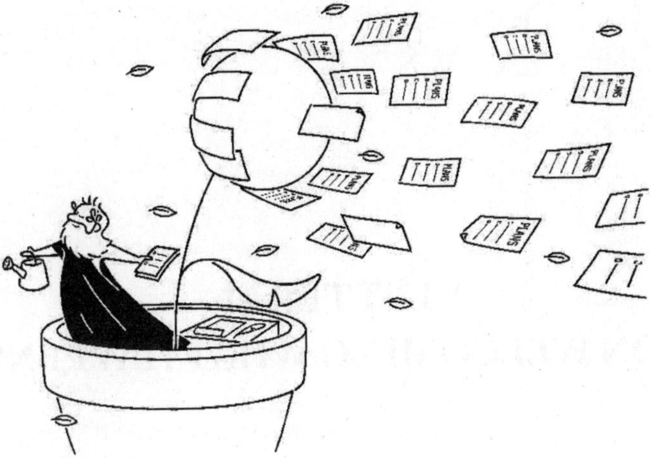
PLANS
PLANS
PLANS
PLANS
PLANS
PLANS
PLANS
PLANS

LETTER 21:
ON WELCOMING WHAT HAPPENS

We've all received weird gifts from people we love. I remember getting a gift card for Six Flags from my college-girlfriend. We hadn't been dating for that long, so she didn't really know me well. I honestly don't like theme parks. I don't know how she came up with the idea, but looking back, I think it's pretty cool. Back then, like an idiot, I immediately frowned when she gave me the gift. She knew I didn't like it. A few days later, I asked her if she could get a refund. If I had the same Stoic mindset back then, I wouldn't have judged the gift so quickly. I would've tried it. Maybe we would have a great day and make some fun memories. You never know.

I was re-reading Marcus Aurelius's *Meditations*. I noticed he talked a lot about accepting whatever happens to you in life. It's one of the main themes of Stoicism. But the Stoics went beyond just accepting external events. Most people prefer 365 days of sunshine, but when it rains, we reluctantly accept it. "Oh no, it's raining again!" We have no other choice than to accept what we don't control: Injuries, loss, the economy, other people's actions, and so forth. But it's all about our attitude towards acceptance. Most of us accept things because we realize there are no other options.

The Stoics accepted things as if they wanted them in the first place. It's a subtle difference, but it has an enormous impact on how you live.

Marcus called this the ability to "practice acceptance without disdain." When you are satisfied with what you have, and accept whatever happens, you no longer struggle with reality. "Why did this happen to me? Why does it rain? Why is there a pandemic? Why can't the vaccine be rolled out faster? Why can't my co-worker respond quicker?" We expend huge amounts of mental energy on things like this. It's a sign that we're either not accepting external events, or we're accepting them with disdain.

We all have this innate drive to mold life. We need to get what we want and we need to avoid what we don't want. But often, the reverse is true. We get what we don't want, and we can't avoid undesirable outcomes.

Don't wish for things to happen the way you like. Instead, welcome whatever happens as if you wanted it to happen. It's a mind trick. And yes, you're basically fooling yourself. But it works. Marcus had some good thoughts on this as well: "Be satisfied with what you have, and accept the present—all of it. And convince yourself that everything is the gift of the gods, that things are good and always will be, whatever they decide and have in store for the preservation of that perfect entity—good and just and beautiful, creating all things, connecting and embracing them, and gathering in their separated fragments to create more like them."

I like the part about convincing yourself that everything is the gift of a higher power—no matter what that is. I must say, this way of looking at the world requires some practice. So if you're thinking this sounds crazy, you're right. I still think it's crazy to treat things you don't want as a gift. But give it a try. You will feel so much more relaxed in life. It's like nothing can harm you.

LETTER 22:
ON PREPARING FOR THE WORST

"New year, new you." It's a silly idea. As if we need to wait with changing ourselves until it's January 1st. Either way, we tend to look forward to the beginning of each year. Somehow we all assume that the new year will be different than last year.

I'm a big fan of Warren Buffett's way of thinking. His firm, Berkshire Hathaway, is most active in the insurance business, and one of their strategies is to plan for the worst. When disasters happen, an insurance company should have enough cash or liquidity to give initial payouts. If they can't do that, they will go under. So what does Buffett plan for? Well, not for one or two disasters to happen, but maybe four at once. Imagine that you have an earthquake in California, a category 5 hurricane in Louisiana, a snowstorm in Minnesota, AND a cyber-attack on the power grid that affects multiple states.

Honestly, it could happen. But there's no need for you and me to get scared right now. Just the thought of multiple disasters happening at the same time will help you to be more clear-headed when things go wrong. And at any time, things can go bad in our lives. In a period of three months, I lost my grandmother, broke up with my girlfriend, quit my job, and moved to a different country. But these periods are simply snapshots in time. It's just like investing.

In March 2020, all tradable asset classes took a major dive. Everything from tech stocks to gold to bitcoin went down. But before the end of the year, almost all indexes recovered, and most assets had new highs that were unthinkable in March.

We just don't know what will happen. It could be positive or negative. Right now, there's a lot of overly optimistic thinking going on. "2021 will be so much better than 2020!" Could be. And my default state of mind is positive. It pays off to be optimistic. But it also could be the case that nothing changes. Sometimes it's good to be a party pooper. I see some people talking about New Year's resolutions as if the pandemic is already behind us. Avoid getting ahead of yourself. Just be at peace with what is.

The Stoics regularly performed thought exercises that helped them prepare for the worst. The primary way of doing that is by reminding yourself of death and loss. They visualized that someone close to them would pass away. It's very effective as a reminder to be more present. But in my experience, this type of negative visualization can also be counterproductive. When you do it too often, you can become numb to it. Or, remembering death can make you feel down if you're already not feeling well. The last thing you want is to get down after doing a Stoic exercise.

I've found another more subtle thought exercise. I learned this from the Buddhist monk, Thich Nhat Hanh. There are actually many similarities between Buddhism and Stoicism. Too much to talk about in this letter. For now, give the following a try.

At different moments during the day (especially when you're overthinking things), say this to yourself: "I am of the nature to have ill health. I cannot escape having ill health."

You might feel good now, but we all deal with some kind of illness during a given year. Maybe you injure your foot (like I did a few days ago), maybe you get the stomach flu, or maybe something worse. Reminding ourselves that things can be bad serves two purposes: First, it reminds us that life is not only rainbows and sunshine. And that setbacks will only make you stronger. But more importantly, preparing for the worst makes you more grateful right now.

Let's give it a try together. Breathe in slowly and say, "I am of the nature to have ill health." Now, breathe out slowly and say, "I cannot escape having ill health." That should snap your right back to the present. Life is better when the present moment is your playground.

LIVING A FULFILLED LIFE

"You act like mortals in all that you fear, and like immortals in all that you desire... [Do not] lose the day in expectation of the night, and the night in fear of the dawn."

— Lucius Annaeus Seneca

LETTER 23:
ON THE BREVITY OF LIFE

I recently caught up with Mike, a former co-worker I used to be very close with. We hadn't talked for three years, but it felt like only yesterday since the last time we met up in London. After our call, I got in a bit of a reflective mood.

Mike and I started our jobs seven years ago on the same day. That's how we became friends; two hungry guys who were trying to climb the corporate ladder. A year and some change later, I left the job to pursue a writing career. But he kept at it. Sometimes you look back at things and think, "Time goes by so fast, it's not funny anymore." It reminded me of Seneca's thoughts on the shortness of life.

He argued that life is not about how long you live, it's about how you use the time that you have. As you know, these Stoic Letters are inspired by Seneca, who said: "Teach me that the good of life does not depend on its length, but its employment, and that it is possible, in fact very often so, that a man who has lived a long time has not lived enough."

Sometimes, we try to get ahead of ourselves by looking at what's in front of us. We look at better times that are ahead.

I'm naturally a person who does that a lot. As a kid, I always dreamed of what my life would look like in the future. And I still think about the future a lot. It gives me the energy and motivation to keep doing my best every single day. But I also need to remind myself that life is not only about tomorrow.

Because if you're too focused on the future, you'll become a person who never has lived enough. That's what Seneca was talking about.

When you always feel like your life is not complete, and something in the future will make you whole, you're never content.

It's one of the toughest paradoxes in life. On the one hand, we need to plan, invest in ourselves, and save money, so we have a better future. But if we put too much weight on our future plans, we risk becoming dependent on them. That's the last thing most of us want.

We want to live a good life—NOW. When death comes knocking, we can't say something like, "Hold on, just give me a few more months, I'm in the middle of starting a new business." That's how most of us go through life—in the middle of something: Getting a degree, buying a house, aiming for a promotion, writing a book, you name it. But we all know we're not going to live forever.

So, what to do? Forget about the future and only live for today? Or plan for the future and forget about today. That's the paradox. And there's not an easy answer to this because life happens in seasons. Sometimes we're more focused on the future, especially when we're going to college, switching careers, coming back from an emotionally draining break up, you name it.

But the majority of our time should be spent on enjoying today. Not because life is short. No, that all depends on your perspective. What matters is that you live well. And funnily enough, we all have an answer to what that exactly means to us. We just need to live according to our definition of it every day. That's a well-lived life.

LETTER 24:
ON LIVING A HAPPY LIFE

What does it take to be happy? Going out with friends? Hanging out at the beach, drinking a mojito? Earning a lot of money? Good health?

Our Stoic friend, Seneca, argued that it was something else. He said: "No one can live happily, or even bearably, without the pursuit of wisdom."

In my experience, this is 100% accurate. That's why I'm surprised people are getting knocked out by the mental toll of the pandemic. Healthy people with jobs and safety complain about how hard life is right now. I can relate to it a bit. But remember that our ancestors went through much harder times than now. And they didn't have the wonders of the modern world. Don't get me wrong, I also wish life was different. But it isn't. Simple as that. Complaining will only make things harder for you. And if you want to be happy, that's the last thing you want to do. The problem is that we have the wrong definition of happiness. What is it?

Going to dinner and a movie? Watching your favorite artist live? Seeing your team play at the stadium? These are just a few of the things I've heard people complaining about not being able to do. Is your attachment to these things worth giving up your happiness for? You and I both know that those things never led to true happiness in the first place. We should trust the advice from the ancient Stoics, who lived in truly hard times. In Ancient Rome, a lot of men didn't live beyond age 30. If I lived back then, I would probably be dead by now. It's a pretty harsh reminder, but it helps me to stay grounded. Life today isn't so bad even with all the challenges we face. So, how can you live happily?

According to the Stoics: Dedicate your life to the pursuit of wisdom. You don't have to be the smartest person in the world. That's not what wisdom is about. It's about having meaning in your life.

It's about waking up every day and getting excited about all the stuff you can learn that day. Isn't that the most exciting thing in the world? You can literally learn about millions of things.

The other day, I watched a documentary called My Octopus Teacher. It's about a relationship between a man and an OCTOPUS. Wait, what? An octopus? Yes, those soft-bodied, eight-legged, alien creatures that swim in the ocean. They became buddies. The man visited his octopus friend every single day for almost a year. Sounds a little weird, and it is, but the film was truly heartwarming. And fascinating too.

That movie exemplifies the importance of the pursuit of wisdom. The man who formed a relationship with the octopus was actually depressed before. Even though he was a family man and did well professionally, he lacked meaning in his life at the time.

But when he discovered his eight-legged underwater friend, he lit up with excitement. He went diving in ice-cold weather through rain, wind, and storms. Didn't matter how he felt. He just wanted to learn everything about the octopus. That can be you too. You don't have to dive into the ocean and befriend a cephalopod. Just learn new things. Immerse yourself in the things that make you curious.

**Dedicate your life to wisdom.
It's the only way to live a consistently happy life.**

And fortunately, the pursuit of wisdom is always available to us—even when we're stuck inside.

LETTER 25:
ON THE HIDDEN VALUE
OF HARD THINGS

Lately, I'm seeing a lot of criticism on the validity of living a productive life. Ever since the height of the Covid pandemic in May of 2020, people have been writing about the dark side of prioritizing your career and work. One of the earliest articles I could find is one called "Is this the end of productivity?" It was really the perfect time for a message like that. So many of us spend our entire lives gunning full force ahead when it comes to working. We tend to go hard until we just physically can't move. That's why we need messages like, "Slow down, you'll be fine if you work a bit less." And yes, it's healthy to remember that you have value as a person outside of your productivity.

It's like your wise grandpa who's saying that you should do everything in moderation. To me, that's still one of the best pieces of advice for a good life, and it's been around for ages. Now, here's the funny thing. Almost two years into this pandemic, people are still preaching you should take it easy all the time. "You're not lazy! You just want to do you. Who needs a career!?" These folks are the opposite of the diehard workaholics, but maybe just as diehard in their beliefs.

The Stoics were always moderate when it came to work and rest. They simply said: Don't overwork. And also don't be lazy, because entropy will take over.

It's just like taking care of your house. If you never clean or maintain it, the house becomes unlivable. Similarly, if we stop taking care of our bodies and minds, we will eventually deteriorate. It's a law of nature.

The truth is we need to do hard things, to maintain equilibrium.

This is a fact we want to ignore because no one likes doing hard things. Who wants to exercise every day? Who wants to work on their relationship and admit they have all kinds of bad habits that originate from their childhood?

Who wants to work all day, building one's career, or perhaps struggling to create a new company together with a bunch of strangers? IT'S HARD. But you and I both know that we need to do those things. Because if we don't, our health, relationships, and lives will only get worse. Nothing in life improves on its own without any form of nurturing. What happens to a plant if you don't give it water? What happens to your car if you don't change the oil? Look, I get why so many people online love to bash productivity culture. It's easy to pick on guys like Gary Vaynerchuck and say, "No, Gary, I don't want to HUSTLE! Take a hike." It feels good to say that kind of stuff just like it feels good to collectively laugh at the high school brain who always stumbles during gym class. The people who are laughing should look at themselves. The critics who are preaching you should rest are often publishing content every single day. They are maybe not aware that being productive also has benefits—especially when you don't overdo it.

The Stoics had a great way of looking at life and work. They always preached doing your best, and nothing less. Epictetus said it without sugar-coating the message: "Don't be lazy and give excuse after excuse. If you continue to do this, your lack of progress may be hidden but, in the end, you will have lived a mediocre life. Decide that you are an adult, and you are going to devote the rest of your life to making progress." They always talked about the importance of doing what's natural as an adult. But here's an important distinction: The Stoics warned us to never look at outcomes. Just like the illustration at the top, look at your next step, not at the finish line—otherwise, you risk slipping on that banana peel. Similarly, if you work hard and you don't get rich, don't give in to disappointment because sometimes things just don't work out. Marcus Aurelius talked about this concept in *Meditations*: "Remember that our efforts are subject to circumstances; you weren't aiming to do the impossible."

At any given time, we're subjected to thousands of external forces that we can't control. We can do work without getting noticed. We can get suddenly ill.

We can lose loved ones. We can get hit with natural disasters. We all know this. And yet, we constantly need to remind ourselves that we don't need to be perfect. When Marcus was talking about how you weren't aiming to do the impossible, he wasn't talking about life in the 21st century, because that's exactly what we're doing.

We aim to have it all. And if we don't get it all, we get down. That's not a good way to live.

It's much better to have no expectations whatsoever. Remember that doing hard work is part of adult life and that the work itself has value, regardless of what rewards we do or don't receive. When you go through life without expecting much from yourself, you can simply do your best, which is enough.

LETTER 26:
ON THE JOY OF
OWNING NOTHING

I like the idea of minimalism. When we own too many things, our lives get cluttered. But if you really think about it, we actually own nothing in life. We're just visitors who get to spend time on this weird planet that spins around in the middle of space.

I sold my car a few weeks ago, and for a moment, I felt a bit sad. But I didn't use my car that much because almost everything I do and need is in my city. I can use any type of transportation to get around, from using my bicycle to grabbing a car or scooter on one of those sharing apps.

When I sold "my" car, I quickly realized it was never my car anyway so there's no need to feel bad. I just got to use it for a few years in exchange for money. You can't lose something you never owned.

I wasn't always like that. When I sold the first car that I bought, I really had to say goodbye. It was emotionally difficult to say goodbye to an object. It sounds weird, but I really felt connected with that car. I had so many good memories of it. The car was there when my first girlfriend and I took a road trip. I drove my first car to the tattoo shop where I got my first tattoo. I drove it to college. The car was there when I had many fun nights out with my friends.

I kept the car for a few years and sold it when I was about 20. The car was so beat up that it cost me hundreds to keep it on the road. I couldn't afford it anymore. But because I was so attached to my car, I couldn't summon the emotional fortitude to sell it myself. I did create the online ad, but I asked my father if he would sell it to the person who wanted to buy the car. I said, "I don't even want to be here when you sell it. I'm going away. When I come back, the car will be gone."

It was really a dramatic scene. I even wrote an article about the car and published it on some hip-hop forums that also published lifestyle blogs. It was one of those early websites that had a combination of news, community, and articles that normal people would submit. The website doesn't exist anymore, but I do remember that I somehow compared my first car to my first girlfriend. She did not like being compared to a car, and now I can definitely understand why. But to my 20-year-old self, it all made sense.

I thought the car was a piece of me. Of course, we know that's nonsense. The Stoic philosopher Epictetus shared really insightful thoughts on this concept. He said: "You cannot really lose anything because you don't own anything in the first place. Not the stuff you have, your spouse, or your property. They are given to you for temporary keep. So never say, 'I have lost something.' You just returned it."

**We really don't own anything.
Even if you live like a minimalist, you still
have no possessions instead of a few possessions.**

That's why I no longer worry about how much stuff I own. It's not something I worry about because I know I actually own nothing. We just get to enjoy things as long we're on this planet. That's not only true for objects, but also for true for people. As Epictetus wrote: "Your spouse died? (S)he was returned." That's probably the most extreme example, but the quote gets the point across. You don't want to make everything about yourself. When we lose people, we think about everything that we are missing, but that's not a good way to think about loss. That doesn't mean the Stoics didn't mourn. They simply had a way to explain death. To have people in our lives is a privilege. Something to not take for granted.

We should enjoy the company of our loved ones and avoid becoming complacent about the time we spend with each other.

At any moment, a person can return to the universe or heaven or whatever you believe in. Epictetus said we should think of all the things in life as a hotel stay. You just don't know exactly when it's time to check out. So never forget to enjoy your stay.

LETTER 27:
ON LIVING A CONSCIOUS LIFE

"It is shameful not to walk but to be carried, and suddenly dazed in the midst of worldly confusion to ask: 'How did I come to this point?'" That's what the Stoic philosopher Seneca wrote in a letter to his good friend Lucilius. Think about it.

Where are you in life? And what led you to this point? Most of us don't have a good answer.

I've learned to ask myself that question all the time: "How did I come to this point?" The first time I asked myself this, it was like a whole new world opened up to me. Until my late twenties, I didn't take enough time to reflect on my decisions. In fact, I didn't even have an answer when I started asking myself that question Seneca posed.

What I found out when I really focused on this question was that many things in my life were an accident. I just stumbled into situations. And I'm not alone: One of the most common answers you get when you ask people "How did you get into this work?" is, "I don't know. I guess it just happened naturally." By naturally, we actually mean it was an accident and we have no clue why we pursued a certain career. In 2010, I started a company in the professional laundry industry with my dad. How did I get into it? My dad was working in that business for two decades. How did he get into it? Totally by accident.

My dad had gone back to school to change careers. He pursued a degree in mechanical engineering and one of his professors knew someone who worked at a large laundry company that served hospitals and other health care institutions. They suggested he try to get a job there, and he did. Now, 30 years later, he's still active in the industry. First as an employee, and now as a business owner.

I have a lot of respect for how my father started with nothing and worked himself up to this point. He went through a lot of shit to get where he is today. But when I asked, "Did you want to get into this industry?", his answer was no. Just like 99% of the population, he had no clue that it even was an industry. In my father's case, it turned out well because he actually became passionate about the laundry business—and still is. He just wanted to have his own company.

I've learned many lessons from my father's story. The most important thing is that you need to love your work. That wasn't true for me in the laundry business. So after four years of working together, I started paving my own path.

I realized that it was a total accident that I got into that industry—and that caused inner frustration. But at the same time, I also didn't know what I really wanted to do.

So many of us are in that weird space. We don't enjoy our work, but we don't know what else we want to pursue.

Through reasoning and reflecting, I realized I needed to make a change. I always enjoyed learning and teaching, but I never wanted to pursue the traditional path. As Seneca said, "From reason, you will learn what to attempt and how; you will not do things by accident." I knew I wanted to do things in my own way instead of working for a school or university.

So I started teaching online classes for motivated professionals, which is something I'm very passionate about. Now and then, I work on my writing class, which I open to students about once or twice a year. It's hard work and requires a lot of energy. But it also gives me pleasure to create new material. And even more, pleasure when my students actually use the material to improve their lives and careers. The other day, one of my students said she started "making sales almost every day while I sleep." That's amazing.

Remember to pave your own path as you make the important decisions in your life. Think things through and make conscious choices. The career you will pursue, the partner you will settle down with, the friends you call your family, the place where you live, etc.

Your life shouldn't be an accident. While most things in life are unexpected, we must continually ask ourselves, "How did I come to this point?"

That's the only way we can guarantee the good life that we actually want.

LETTER 28:
ON THE SHORT TIME
YOU HAVE LEFT

Whether you're 25 or 85, it always seems like you have a short time left. When you're 85, you still have so many things you didn't have the chance to do. If you have grandkids, you want to see them grow up, and have their own kids. When you're 25, you have so many desires and things you still want to do, that even 200 years of life wouldn't be enough. There is always something left to do, regardless of your age.

This is something the philosopher and emperor Marcus Aurelius also recognizes when he wrote, "Only a short time left," in his journal when he was reigning the largest empire at the time.

His solution to dealing with that harsh reality? "Live as if you were alone—out in the wilderness. No difference between here and there: the city that you live in is the world. Let people see someone living naturally, and understand what that means."

What does it mean? Unfortunately he didn't give us a detailed explanation of what it means to live "naturally." But by reading his other thoughts, my interpretation of "nature" according to Marcus Aurelius is to be one with the world you're experiencing. Let's break down what that means. If you look at your own fear of death, what do you see? You probably have all these things you still want to do before you die, right? Places to visit, things to learn, goals to accomplish, and so forth.

This constant desire for things means that there's a difference between here (the present) and there (the future). "Here" is where you are right now. Your current state. Whether that's rich or poor, in shape or out of shape, experienced traveler or not. "There" is where you want to be.

There's a space between those two states. Most of life is spent in that space. And that's a really bad place to be because you're stuck between now and the future. Isn't that sad? We keep living our lives in "the space" and we are never really here. We just rush the present so we can get to the future.

I think that's what Marcus meant when he said, "No difference between here and there." Where you live is the world. In other words: No matter where you are or what you do, it's the only thing you have at that moment. So make sure you get the most out of it. As Marcus also put it, live as if you were alone in the wilderness. Because when you're in the wilderness, you don't daydream about some kind of perfect future when you will be happy or satisfied. Your only focus is on what's right in front of you. But so many of us are in this lifelong waiting room.

We're waiting until we have the perfect job, house, relationship, degree, and so forth.

But as we're waiting, we keep on wasting today. Keep doing that every day, and you end up wasting a life. How can we avoid that? By not being in a nonstop rush. This is counterintuitive if we realize that we don't live forever. The natural reaction is to hurry, right? It's like going bowling with your friends. For the first few games, you take it easy and get in a flow. But when your time is almost up at the hour, and the next group is eagerly breathing in your neck, you lose all the excitement and fun of the game. You just want to wrap up the game in a hurry so you can move on. Avoid living your life like that.

Don't hurry everything you do today so you can just get it over with. What kind of life is that?

Enjoy the moment! Because no matter how much time you have left, it's actually enough.

BUILDING A BETTER
VERSION OF YOURSELF

**"Progress is not achieved by luck or accident, but
by working on yourself daily."**

— Epictetus

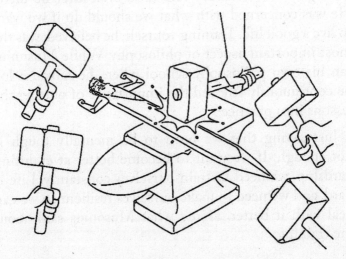

LETTER 29:
ON THE VALUE OF TRAINING
YOUR MIND AND BODY

One of the lesser-known Stoic philosophers is Musonius Rufus, who was the mentor of Epictetus. He was one of the most popular and famous philosophers in Rome during the first century AD (and even after he died). He was concerned with what we should do if we want to live a good life. Training yourself, he believed, was the most important aspect of philosophy. While Musonius ran his own philosophy school where he talked a lot, he continuously stressed the importance of putting the lessons into practice.

Just saying that we need to be mentally tough is not enough. If we want to become better at enduring hardship, we need to train ourselves constantly. Life is hard, and we need to make ourselves resilient so we can deal with it better. Here's what Musonius said about the training:

> **"We will train both soul and body when we accustom ourselves to cold, heat, thirst, hunger, scarcity of food, hardness of bed, abstaining from pleasures, and enduring pains."**

Training is an important aspect of philosophy. The Stoics realized that just like we regularly train our bodies, we need to keep training our minds to stay focused on living a good life. We can't expect to read about a few life lessons and then always live by them. I don't know about you, but I find that I frequently forget about what leads to a good life.

When I don't remind myself of it enough, I might stop meditating, reading books, and enjoying the smaller things in life. It's the same way with my strength and stamina. If I don't train, I slowly lose my physical capabilities. I know, I wish we could train a few times and then keep our gains forever. But neither body nor mind has that power. I love how Seneca shared advice for fitness with his friend Lucilius: "There are easy and quick exercises which tire the body out quickly and save time, which we should particularly keep in mind; running and moving the arms with weights, and jumping, either the high jump that lifts the body." It's hard to imagine there were fitness programs in Ancient Rome, but they really valued staying in shape. But Seneca also said: "Whatever you do, come back quickly from the body to the mind; exercise the mind night and day. It is nourished by a moderate effort." That's the key. Moderate effort.

Only when you exert moderate effort can you maintain your strength, and potentially grow stronger.

This is true for the body and the mind. When you've acquired Stoic wisdom, it's important that you maintain that wisdom. Keep reading about the philosophy. Keep reminding yourself of the principles. That's the only way to maintain it. And if you learn new things as you go, that's great too. In fact, it's highly likely you keep learning new things whether you like it or not. It's the same thing with the body. I know that society is all about "bigger, better, stronger," but that's not a realistic goal. It's much more realistic to say: "I'm going to get strong, and then I'm going to stay strong. I don't need to be stronger."

I get the whole mantra of doing more, improving by 1 per cent, and being just a little bit better. But you and I both know that's not sustainable. Even if we push ourselves a little bit every day, we soon reach a wall. When that happens, we stop. And then, we lose our wisdom or strength. That's something you can avoid by aiming to maintain whatever you have. Like the Stoics, focus on a moderate effort. There's nothing wrong with that. In fact, a moderate effort has helped me to build a sustainable career. I kept doing just a little bit year in year out. Everything compounds.

LETTER 30:
ON LIVING A RESOURCEFUL LIFE

Have you noticed how quickly we become accustomed to the things we have in our lives? We all have our objects we think we can't live without. When I'm at home, I generally wear several pairs of shoes during the week. I have my favorite pair for running, another one for going on a walk, a pair I like to wear when I lift weights, and a few pairs for social situations. But when I go on a trip or a vacation, I can't bring all the shoes I like to wear.

When I go away with a suitcase, I usually wear my favorite sneakers and I'll bring a pair of running shoes. Before I leave, I always think, "I wish I could bring everything I need." But as soon as I arrive, I realize that I actually don't need that much to do exactly the same things I do at home. It's not just shoes, of course. This is true of many of the things we think we need—and it's something Seneca explained well. He said: "Until we have begun to go without them, we fail to realize how unnecessary many things are. We've been using them not because we needed them but because we had them."

Think about it. How many things in your life can you classify like that? I know it's difficult to imagine a life without your favorite mug or any other thing you've grown accustomed to, but once you leave your home, you'll realize you can continue to live well. If you think you need a whole laundry list of items you "can't live without," you're giving material objects too much power.

The only things we really can't live without are the basics—water, food, shelter. Other things are optional. When you live your life focusing on material objects, two things happen.

You don't get attached to objects: Sometimes things like jewelry, shoes, clothes, or your favorite mug become part of your identity. But we're not defined by what we own. These are simply things we temporarily have in our lives. You will feel grateful for what you do have: Janet Jackson (and Joni Mitchell) was spot on when she sang "you don't know what you've got til it's gone." She of course talked about a lover, but it's really true across the board. When the things you rely on are (temporarily) out of your life, you realize that you didn't appreciate them enough. That should serve as a reminder to be grateful today for what you do have.

One of the biggest benefits I've experienced from Stoicism is that philosophy makes you resourceful. In life, it's not about what we have, it's about what we do with the things we do have.

As I'm writing this, the economy is very unstable. It seems as if our economy is like a ruler that's balancing on a finger. It goes all over the place. The only thing it's not is stable.

When I speak to entrepreneurs and investors, I hear two types of thinking. People are either worried about all of the risks (and there are a lot of them) and yet keep doing what they are doing, or they are already preparing themselves for a downturn. The latter group is willing to do whatever it takes to adapt, while the former group feels uncomfortable with change. The other day I was talking to a business owner in his sixties. We were talking about the possibility of a recession and bear market that lasts for years, not months. "I'll work a few extra years or tighten my belt. I'll do whatever," he said defiantly.

To have that type of Stoic fortitude, we need to train ourselves. That type of willingness to do whatever it takes only comes from taking action for years. It's not something you build in a year or two. It takes decades. That might sound offputting, but it's 100% worth it. If the business owner I was talking to didn't build self-confidence throughout his life, I bet he wasn't that defiant right now.

He would be worried out of his mind.

But instead, he has something that many people don't have: Resourcefulness.

The ability to find creative and realistic ways to overcome difficulties. Start practicing now with small things and you'll thank yourself later when that resourcefulness comes in handy.

LETTER 31:
ON THE VALUE OF
MAKING MISTAKES

There are many mistakes you can avoid in life without having to learn the hard way. I don't have to lose all my money in the stock to learn that stock picking doesn't end well for the majority. I can read about the most common investing mistakes and avoid them. You can say the same about many things, from building relationships to starting a business.

But there are also many mistakes we can't avoid, no matter how hard we try. You can read all about human nature, study psychology—and yet, you can get fooled by a charlatan. You can watch endless YouTube videos with tips about avoiding injuries, and yet, you can get injured. Last week, I injured my back. It was completely my own fault. I had been working out more than usual, and on top of that, I also traveled. I simply put more physical stress on my body than usual. And I didn't consider the correct posture. I didn't really do my daily stretches for a few days before I got injured.

The funny thing is that I blew out my back when I came back to my parents after traveling. I was feeling really good physically. When I grabbed my parent's cat, a British shorthair by the name of Archibald, I felt a sting in my lower back, on the left side.

It was the same area I've had issues with since I was 16. I hadn't had any real back problems for about 10 years. But I made a few small mistakes and boom, my back went out. I couldn't stand up straight. It's been five days now, and it's better, but it was pretty bad.

I saw it as a time to reflect on my habits, and as a reminder that small mistakes build up. Sure, I could've avoided this by sticking to my good posture and avoiding too much physical stress around the time I was traveling. But I learned a lesson: If you ignore your good habits, you'll pay for them. Every time I make a mistake, I see it as an opportunity to rethink other important things in my life. Am I spending enough time with my friends and family? Do I keep enriching my mind? Do I stay in shape? What about my diet? And sleep?

You can do a check-in with yourself regularly. Even if you do this once a year, you make sure you're on the right path.

As Seneca once said, we keep learning as we keep living: "As long as you live, keep learning how to live to err is human, but to persist (in the mistake) is diabolical." Learning how to live is a deeply personal matter. We have to learn what works for us. And we can only do that by living a conscious life. Isn't that how philosophy started, with Socrates when he said, "The unexamined life is not worth living"? As long as you live, keep examining yourself. When you make a mistake, don't get bogged down. Learn from it somehow.

LETTER 32:
ON MASTERING THE SKILL
OF SELF TALK

When you're healthy all your life and suddenly experience recurring pain because of a condition or injury, it doesn't only affect you physically, but also mentally. I've been dealing with post-infectious IBS for two years now.

I experience severe bouts of stomach pain that last somewhere between days to weeks. My self-talk initially was like any other time I would get the flu or short-term injury: "Just get some rest. Take it easy. Don't work out much. It will pass."

This was a passive mindset, accepting the condition. But when my health problem didn't disappear, that mindset became harmful. I was being too passive. Sometimes, you let life happen to you. That's what happened with my stomach problems as well. About two months ago, I decided I'd had enough. I changed my self-talk.

**In life, I don't believe we can afford to be passive.
I believe in addressing life head-on.**

I believe that a proactive mindset works best: mentally, physically, and professionally. Now I say: "I don't care about the stomach pain. I'm going to work through it. I'm not going to give up and lay in bed at the first sign of pain. I'll fight."

I'm talking to the pain there. And that head-on works for me because it gives me energy. This doesn't mean everyone has to do the same. The point is that you have the power to change your self-talk if you want. If you feel like the voice in your head is somehow standing in the way of living a good life, realize that you can change the voice. We don't have to give in to emotions, pain, weakness, and our innate drive to pursue the path of least resistance. We as humans have the power to reason with ourselves. This is one of the foundational beliefs of Stoicism. As Seneca once said:

"You are a reasoning animal. So what is the good in you? Perfect reason. So call it back on duty to pursue its goal, and let it grow abundantly, as much as it is able."

When you're dealing with negative or unhelpful self-talk, you have the ability to use reason to make a change. While the perfect reason is an unattainable goal, the point of Stoicism is to aspire to be as close to perfect as possible. No one expects you to always live according to Stoic values and be positive, resilient, and never have a moment of weakness. That's not realistic. But trying to be your best and most reliable self is very realistic.

Never forget that we're stronger than we think. We can persevere through difficulty even though our minds always prefer comfort. I really experienced that with my IBS. The more I give in comfort, the more pain I experienced. When I don't exercise and take it really easy, I always have more stomach pain. Exercise improves my gut health. Running is also very effective in improving my gut problems. When I experience stomach cramps and bloating, it's really uncomfortable to run. But after about 20 to 25 minutes, I start feeling better. I learned what works well for me through trial and error.

Now, this obviously not the case with all conditions. The more proactive I am, the better I feel. And I'm pain-free for a while. Looking back, I now think that's obvious. But when you feel weak, your instinct is to stay put. Now, my goal is to keep working out and stay mentally tough. Even if we know we'll never be perfect, or totally free of pain or problems, just like the Stoics, we can aim for the perfect. No one ever got worse by trying to be better.

LETTER 33:
ON THE "SECRET"
TO BECOMING BETTER

I've been thinking a lot about the difference between acquiring wisdom versus executing wisdom. I always dedicate a lot of time to study, no matter what's going on in the world. And I enjoy the activity of reading—not just the purpose like learning or entertaining yourself. I've noticed that I spent more time merely consuming information. And I'm not alone. We're all trying to make sense of everything that's going on right now. We read about history, philosophy, psychology, and any other field that could give us some wisdom so we at least feel better.

But all of this "sense-making" only leads to more knowledge, and less execution. And as you and I both know, more knowledge by itself is not useful. What do you want to do with all that information that you're putting in your mind? It's time to execute! "That's great, Darius. But how on earth can I execute when I'm stuck at home." That is what you're probably thinking right now. I get it. So let me explain what I mean.

**First, start seeing yourself as an athlete.
Your job is to perform in this game called life.
And to perform, you need two things:
A plan, and stamina.**

You create your plan based on the wisdom you've acquired. At some point, we all know what it takes to have a good life and career. It's the usual: Take care of yourself, sleep enough, don't take things too seriously, laugh a little, meditate, be kind to your loved ones, show compassion, avoid short-term gratification, etc. There's nothing complicated about that.

Most of us are good at creating a plan. But we lack stamina. So what happens? We struggle. "Why am I feeling down? Why am I stuck in my career?" Well, you know what it takes! You just need some stamina to pull through.

Now we just need to figure out how to improve our stamina. Actually, we don't need to figure out anything. This is something you know as well. How do you improve your physical stamina? What do runners do? What do athletes do every day of their lives?

That's right, they train. Ideally, with a master, coach, or someone who's been there. Marcus Aurelius, once the most powerful man in the West, humbly said: "Mastery of reading and writing requires a master." He might have talked about a skill like writing, but this is true when it comes to everything.

We all need to train our skills and mind to improve our mental stamina. The good thing about our digital age is that you don't have to know a master personally. You can learn through books, articles, courses, podcasts, etc. For example, one of the masters I've learned writing from is William Zinsser. He passed away in 2015, and I never met him. But I still studied with him through his books.

The key is to train in a mindful way. Don't just learn things. Turn everything you learn into an activity.

For example, to train inner tranquility, meditate, or go for a long walk without getting distracted by your thoughts. To become a better speaker, dictate your journal entries. To become a better writer, design your day in a way that's easy for you to write. You can't expect to improve or to stay at a certain level without proper training. It's like eating, bathing, and breathing: It's a continuous practice.

Ernest Hemingway also knew that the "secret" to becoming better is to train. He once said: "It's none of their business that you have to learn to write. Let them think you were born that way." It's a secret that's not a secret. We all know what it takes to become better. We need to execute.

Once you've improved, people will look at you
and think, "Wow, this person got their
shit together!" Know that you've trained
yourself to get to that point.

Once you've improved, people will look at you
and think, "Wow, this person got their
shit together." Know that you've trained
yourself to get to that point.

LETTER 34:
ON TRYING TO BECOME
STRONGER EVERY DAY

When I started writing online, I looked at people who
had a hundred thousand followers on social media or
in their newsletter, and thought, "Wow, their writing
careers must be so much easier than mine."

This type of thinking is common. I've heard it from
many friends and colleagues. We often look at one
particular thing that someone has and assume that their
entire life must be so much better than ours.

- "If I had a bigger house, I would be so much
  happier at home."

- "If I had a better car, I would visit so many
  places."

- "If I had five hundred thousand followers, I would
  post more content."

But how do you know for certain that life will be so
much better when you acquire something? Will life be
any different if you have 100K followers?

I can tell you from personal experience that my life isn't any different than five years ago. Look, things are certainly easier when you have more money, reach, or a bigger network. But those things usually come because you've done the work. When you leave out the people who are born into wealth or status, you see that money or recognition usually comes because a person did something. For example:

- When you build a successful business, you usually make a lot of money.

- When you're really good at a particular skill, you are handsomely rewarded for performing that skill.

- When you can entertain people so well that they forget about the problems in their lives, or teach them something crucial, maybe you will amass a lot of followers.

We tend to focus on the rewards: The money, recognition, followers, status. But when we do this, we forget the action that leads to the rewards: Building the business; mastering the skill; rehearsing the entertainment. This is something we all know. But here's an even more important thing. The REAL reward you acquire is not the money or status, it's the energy, pride, and sense of accomplishment you get from performing the action.

Let me tell you why I started writing and why I'm still writing: Every time I write something I'm passionate about, I feel fantastic when I'm writing, and also when I'm finished writing. It's difficult but satisfying work.

To me, this is the real secret to living a happy, energetic, and good life. It's about finding those activities that you love and that improve your life. Seneca recommended doing something every day that improves you, and giving it all your attention:

"Each day acquire something that will fortify you against poverty, against death, indeed against other misfortunes as well; and after you have run over many thoughts, select one to be thoroughly digested that day."

Can we honestly say we're doing that every day? Or are we getting distracted by the shiny things we see? The number of followers, expensive car, big house, fancy jet-set lifestyle, or blue checkmark on social media? Those are not things we should look at for happiness or satisfaction.

We should only look at the actions that usually lead to good things.

And even if you aim to become the best at your job, but don't get famous, so what? At least you do what Seneca said. You're acquiring skills and strength that will strengthen so you take on the challenges of life. That's worth more than money or fame.

LETTER 35:
ON BEING FORGIVING
TOWARDS YOURSELF

I just came back from a three-week trip to Barcelona. I planned to stay in the city for longer, but I decided to cut the trip short because I started having stomach pain. Instead of pushing through the pain, I came back home to The Netherlands to see my doctor. I probably caught a stomach virus or bacteria. While the trip to Barcelona was good, it was also stressful. I had planned it full of activities and tasks because I wanted to see whether I could live there. I put a lot of pressure on the trip to succeed. I wanted to discover different neighborhoods, look at apartments, connect with locals, and also keep up my normal habits like working out, running, and writing.

When my stomach pain started popping up after two weeks in Spain, my initial response was one of self-criticism. "Why did you plan so much stuff? Why did you book an apartment that's so far from the neighborhoods you actually like?" Thoughts like these are useless, but we all have them. The truth is we're not perfect geniuses who do everything flawlessly. We make mistakes. Life throws us curveballs. Isn't that the nature of life?

Stomach pain is not new to me since I have irritable bowel syndrome, which is often inconvenient and sometimes painful, but usually fine to live with. But when I experience stress, good or bad, I have more gut problems. So I have even more incentive to manage stress. But I'm still human and experience stressful situations. No matter what you do, you will always have problems. If you're rich, you have rich people's problems. If you have a job, you have employed people problems. If you're self-employed, you have self-employed problems. Same with relationships. Single people complain about being alone. People in relationships complain they don't have enough personal space.

When we experience setbacks or when things do go the way we want, we have a tendency to find someone to blame.

Why is that? Why must there be someone to point the finger to and say, "IT'S ALL YOUR FAULT"? Epictetus once shared an important lesson about blame: "When we are frustrated, angry, or unhappy, let's hold ourselves responsible for these emotions because they are the result of our judgments. No one else is responsible for them. When you blame others for your negative feelings, you are being ignorant. When you blame yourself for your negative feelings, you are making progress. You are being wise when you stop blaming yourself or others."

Some people read that and think we should blame ourselves because we're responsible. But that's not what Epictetus meant. He meant you should take responsibility for your negative feelings. When you blame yourself, you generate animosity toward yourself. So when things don't go your way, and you're blaming yourself or others, remember the words of Epictetus. It's always foolish to blame yourself for things that happen in life. Even if you think something is 100 per cent your fault, it's not wise to punish yourself by thinking about what you should've done differently. Sure, you could have done things differently. But you didn't, and you don't have a time machine—and that's fine. It's time to move on because life is too short to beat yourself up!

The reality is that most things in life are not fully our fault. I'm not saying we shouldn't take personal responsibility. But when you do your best and things just don't work out, simply accept the outcome. I went to Barcelona, planned to do a million things, learned that I didn't judge things correctly, got ill, and cut the trip short. I didn't stay there so I could "power through." Some things are not worth it. I knew that pushing myself would only have a negative effect on my health, so why do it?

Your physical and mental health are always more important. So make sure you always do the thing that's in the best interest of those two things.

LETTER 36:
ON STRIVING FOR BETTERMENT

"It doesn't matter how good a life you've led. There'll still be people standing around the bed who will welcome the sad event." That's what Marcus Aurelius wrote when he was Emperor of Rome. For a person in power, it's obvious to feel the heat of the enemies who'd rather have the power themselves.

But you don't have to be an emperor to have people in your life who don't wish you the best. I also have family members who'd rather see me fail. It's a part of life. I've never met a successful person who didn't experience jealousy and hate from people close to them.

The other day I was talking to a long-time friend who I've known since I was 15. We used to play on the same basketball team. He mentioned that he lost touch with a lot of his best friends of that era. In recent years they started to distance themselves from my friend. You know how it goes. First, you don't get invited to social gatherings, then you're no longer welcome at birthdays, and finally, there's no contact whatsoever anymore.

While this was several years ago, my friend was still upset about not seeing those guys anymore. "I really don't get it. We were such good friends. They never said why they stopped inviting me. What's up with that?"

Well, sometimes people just have no reason. The time that friendship started to fade was when my friend got serious about his education. He changed careers several years ago, got a degree, and works as a health care professional in psychiatric care. Those guys never changed. They still have the exact same life. And they never seem happy somehow.

When you have a different lifestyle than others, they think you're weird. I experienced the exact same thing when I went to graduate school. My old drinking buddy friends and I just stopped talking to each other. In my case, it was completely mutual. I strived to make my life better. And they didn't care about betterment. I knew they didn't wish me well. Instead of encouraging me to continue my studies, they tried to persuade me to go out clubbing instead of studying. I wasn't interested.

Ignore the people who judge you and celebrate when you fail. But no matter how nasty and jealous others can be, Marcus Aurelius warned us not to be like them: "And yet, don't leave angry with them. Be true to who you are: caring, sympathetic, kind."

To uplift my friend, I shared those words with him. I said I admired his dedication and intentions. We need people who are serious about themselves and are just as serious about helping others.

The best thing we can do is to never be like the negative people on this planet. There will always be people who would rather see you stay where you are. They want you to be like them, so they have company. Don't let that negativity spoil your soul. Stay true to who you are.

LETTER 37:
ON THE BENEFITS OF
ANNOYING THINGS

The Stoic Musonius Rufus believed that "the soul is strengthened as it is trained for courage by enduring hardships and trained for self-control by abstaining from pleasures."

I wonder what he would think of today's world that is obsessed with comfort. We do everything to be more comfortable. I'm guilty of this as well. Last year I bought a heated mattress pad for cold winter nights. To me, that's now the symbol of extreme comfort.

When I read Musonius' work, I'm reminded that hardship is good. I find it highly annoying to be cold, but enduring annoying times only strengthens you. Not in a physical way because no matter how much I expose myself to cold, I still find it annoying. I might build some tolerance, but I don't have the same genes as Nordic people.

However, enduring hardship makes my mind harder. There are many luxurious things in life I purposefully avoid. I can afford to buy a bigger house for a few years now, but I still live in the same house I bought in 2017, which is considered small by most standards. I also avoid buying exotic food and fruit every single week. Most of the time I stick to simple food. Not because I can't afford it but because I can live well on simple food. All of this is training for life. In fact, it's living and training at the same time.

I want to avoid getting too comfortable. While I don't care about the alleged benefits of cold showers, I sometimes shower from start to finish with cold water. All of this training gives you true comfort. When you're accustomed to basic conditions, you will walk with a sense of calmness through life. You won't be afraid to lose everything you have because you're living simply anyway. Musonius explained this paradox well:

"The first step in the proper training of the soul is to keep handy the proofs showing that things which seem to be good are not good and that things which seem to be bad are not bad, and to become accustomed to recognizing things that are truly good and distinguishing them from things that are not."

We're made to believe that hardship is bad and that pleasure is good. The Stoics always challenged this idea. They flipped things around. Hardship is good. Too much pleasure is bad. Of course, life doesn't have to be one long endurance event that's full of hardship and deprivation.

The beauty of Stoicism is that pleasure, rest, and comfort feel so much better when you do have them. I still like pleasure. And to be honest, I still like my heated pad. I just don't use it all the time. But when I do, man, it feels good!

II.
THE OUTER WORLD

Happiness is not only being able to live well with yourself. That's the foundation. But we're part of a larger ecosystem. We have to find a way to be comfortable in society as well since we're social beings. While it might seem like an attractive idea to distance yourself from the world and only focus on your mental health, it's not realistic or practical.

Stoic wisdom is about finding ways to deal with the challenges of being part of society. With these strategies, you will not only feel mentally strong, but you will also find a way to thrive in society.

PURSUING WORLDLY SUCCESS

"It is in virtue that happiness consists, for virtue is the state of mind which tends to make the whole of life harmonious."

— Zeno of Citium

LETTER 38:
ON THE PRICE WE PAY TO GET
WHAT WE WANT

In life, there are many ongoing games. For example, one of the biggest games on earth is the career game. If you want to play that game, you need to obey the rules. You need to get your degrees, apply for jobs, put on your game face, hide your personality, please your bosses, go to their birthday parties, and so forth. If you play the game well, your reward is status and money. But here's something most people forget.

You pay a price to play a game.

When it comes to your career, you might have to give up your morals, values, and time that you otherwise would've spent on family, friends, or hobbies. It's a high price that you pay. And when people don't think about what they sacrifice to succeed at the career game, it can lead to inner conflict. The Stoic philosopher Epictetus related an example about personal relationships.

He said: "If you are not invited to a party maybe it is because you didn't pay the price, such as flattering the host or doing things to be in her good books. So if you want to be invited, pay the bill and don't complain about the cost. But if you expect the benefits without paying the price you are not only greedy, you are being foolish. What if you are not invited to the party? You did not do things you didn't want to do such as flattering the host. You have the advantage of not compromising your integrity."

Not complaining about the price we pay is the key to happiness.

Take Epictetus' example. If you begrudgingly pay the price for being in someone's good books, you only end up with inner conflict. Maybe you're only nice to someone because they are a co-worker and you can't stand being alone for a minute. So you say yes to everything the other person asks for: You do their dirty work, you help them with moving, laugh at their not-funny jokes. You do everything so you're not excluded. But what's so bad about being excluded from silly things?

When I had my first job at a bank many years ago, I thought I needed to please everyone I worked with. So I was always part of the social situations during lunch breaks and all the after-work events. It was a lot of fun. But one thing I couldn't stand was all the gossip. It sucked me in, and after a while, I noticed myself gossiping as well. I couldn't understand that one moment people were nice to someone, and it looked like we were all best friends, and another moment, when that person wasn't there, everyone talked about their sex life and bad traits. And I definitely couldn't understand why I was doing the same thing so quickly.

But I do understand it better now. It's human nature to gossip and to be attracted to pleasure. But I never felt good about those things. So when I stepped away from the group slowly and stopped laughing at their jokes, I wasn't invited to their social situations and birthdays anymore. It was the best thing that happened to me at that time in my life.

Instead of filling my time with gossip and bullshit, I focused on my education, sports, and true friends. I decided to play a different game. One that's driven by an inner scorecard.

This is something that the Stoics did well. They promoted staying true to your values. If you can stay true to what you think is important and still play a game, then go ahead. For example, Stoics can still pursue wealth and money as long as they don't sacrifice their values. But the moment you have to exchange your values for money, you always come to the same conclusion: It's just not worth it. Your values are priceless.

LETTER 39:
ON THE BIGGEST PRIZE
IN LIFE

To desire pleasure is to accept pain. Because at some point, you become addicted to whatever is giving you pleasure. But when you desire nothing you can be emotionally free. Seneca said it best: "If I yield to pleasure, I shall have to yield to pain, I shall have to yield to toil and to poverty. Ambition and anger want the same rights over me; I shall be pulled, even torn apart, between so many emotions. Liberty is the prize. This is the reward of toil. You ask what is liberty? To be enslaved to no object, no necessity, no chances, to reduce fortune to a level field? The day I realize I have more power than she, she will have no more power."

Freedom is the biggest prize in life. And I'm not only talking about living in a free country, which is something everyone who lives in freedom should cherish every single day. When the Stoics talked about emotional freedom, they meant not being enslaved to mental constructs.

In more recent times, the wrongly imprisoned boxer Rubin "Hurricane" Carter embodied that mindset in real life. When Hurricane Carter was sentenced to life in prison after being framed for a crime he didn't commit, he remained free in his own mind. He never looked at himself as a person who lived in captivity. That mindset helped him to stay positive and focused on proving his innocence.

Tragically, he spent almost 20 years in prison. Carter might have physically been in prison, but his mind remained free from anger, negativity, and revenge. Bob Dylan, inspired by Carter's story, even wrote an 8-minute song about the story (it's called Hurricane and it's really good). Denzel Washington portrayed Carter in a movie about his life, which is also great.

As Seneca remarked 2000 years ago, to be free is to not give power to fortune. In life, many things happen to us, starting with birth. We have no control over what family we're born into. According to the Stoics, those circumstances are all up to fortune. They believed that our purpose in life is to break from what fortune pushes on us.

To obtain freedom, the biggest prize in life, we should realize that we always have the power to decide how to live. We might not be able to change life's events, but we can certainly change how we look at them.

That mindset reminds me of the author and podcaster Jocko Willink, who has a philosophy that he calls "good." When anything happens to him, he looks at the positive side. He flips things around and looks at how he can use that event to his advantage. For example, he says, "Hurt? Sick? Injured? Lack of time? Tired? Lack of resources? Hungry? Thirsty? Not feeling 100 per cent? GOOD. DO WHAT YOU CAN."

Focus on what you control and be free. This is the mindset that leads to real personal freedom. No matter what happens in life, you will be okay. When you can go through life that way, nothing will have the power to hold your mind captive. You will have freedom. When you have nothing, everything else in life is a bonus.

LETTER 40:
ON THE EXCESSIVE DESIRE
FOR SUCCESS

What is it that you're after this year? A higher paycheck? A new house? More friends? Building a business? As you're getting after it, remind yourself to stay focused on the journey—not the outcome.

Everything you want in life has a price. That's something we tend to forget. We get stuck in what I call, "but if I" thinking. We say stuff like, "I know it takes a lot of effort to get what I want. But if I get it, I will be happy." If you get too caught up in the things you want to accomplish this year, you might end up paying a high price.

How often have you sacrificed your inner peace for some sort of success? We tend to look at the outcomes, like a higher salary, degree, better job title, and hardly ever look at the price we have to pay to obtain those things.

When I got out of grad school, I wanted to earn 100K a year. Where did that come from? I honestly have no clue.

Our society has an obsession with round numbers, especially starting with one, followed by at least six figures, and preferably seven.

Anyway, I had to make that number per year to be satisfied with my career. As I was pursuing success, I felt I was always close to burn-out. And deep inside, I knew that was only the start.

What happens once you make 100K? "Let me try to get more!" It's the same old song: More, more, more. Oh, I wish I had more!

I don't think we're all born greedy. It's a trap that many of us fall into. It's simply a matter of a carrot on a stick. You chase what you don't have. And that's what I did as well. But at some point, I decided to think more about the price I pay for success. And let's face it, success, money, fame, it's all great. But nothing is worth your happiness, peace, and tranquility.

Now, you might think, "But if I'm rich, life will be easier!" That's a classic example of "but if I" thinking. Why do you think that? It's really not true. How often have you chased something to only figure out that nothing changed once you got it? It starts when we go to college. "When I graduate, it will be sooo easy to find a job." Nope.

It's the same with success and money. One of our family friends is very wealthy, as in 100 million dollars wealthy. He once said something like, "Being rich is not that great." Everybody assumes that's what only entitled rich people say. That's true. But when I asked why he thinks that, he said that at any given time, he's dealing with multiple lawsuits, employees at his companies who did something illegal, family members who want something, and so forth. He's always dealing with stress-inducing situations. Is that something you want? Most of us just want to take the money.

"Mo money, mo problems" is what Biggie rapped. You're not so much better off if you have a lot of money or success. Mentally speaking, you're worse off because success brings problems and breeds greed.

This is one of the main points of the Stoics. They argued that all great things come at a price. Seneca himself was a highly successful person in Ancient Rome. For the most part of his life, he had money, respect, and status—so he talked from experience. But he also had wisdom. He knew that nothing comes cheap.

Seneca said: "Success is greedy and exposed to the greed of others; as long as nothing is sufficient for you, you will not be enough for others." Even if you don't have mo problems, you'll have mo greed.

So next time you admire that perfect-looking Instagram celebrity, take a few minutes to meditate on the blessings of your own life. Understand that the lives of the rich and famous are really not that great. What matters is that you live according to your values. And most importantly, you enjoy the time you have on this planet, floating in the middle of space, surrounded by nothing. It's fascinating when you think about it.

We're so busy worrying about being successful that we miss the mundane miracles that happen around us every day. Enjoy your journey—no matter what the circumstances or outcomes are.

LETTER 41:
ON REACHING YOUR GOALS

Here's how I used to set goals for myself. I looked at what kind of outcome I desired and then set a goal to achieve that thing. When it came to my career, I always looked at how much money I wanted to make. So my goals looked like this: "I want to make $100K a year." And when it came to my health, it would be this: "I want to put on 5 pounds of muscle." That stuff never works. Can you relate to that?

How often have you been frustrated by your own goals? You set goals, things don't go as you expected, and then you give up. How is that helping?

No wonder so many people have a huge aversion to goals. One of my friends once said, "just the thought of setting goals reminds me of those Tony Robbins disciples who walk on fire. Not my thing." I think Tony is great. But you really don't need to do fist bumps and hit your chest to get pumped up about life. All of that bro behavior makes me cringe too. The problem is that we often set bad goals. And when we do that, we actually set ourselves up for failure. No wonder we fail to reach our goals.

I've found that you can use Stoicism to reach your goals more effectively. What does that look like? You set goals that are within your control. And instead of looking at outcomes, you look at actions. Let me give you an example. I still have the ambition to earn more in my career. To me, it's a sign that you're doing something well. The more value you create for others, the more you will be rewarded for it. Just because I follow Stoic principles, it doesn't mean I denounce wealth.

Instead, I focus on the work I need to do that could result in a certain income. If I do mediocre work, spend my evenings watching TV, plan my weekends full of leisure, I know damn straight that my income will not increase. But if I create value in the form of books, articles, courses, coaching, I know I have more odds of earning more. If I invest my money in real estate and stocks, it's the same. I focus on the actions. And I do all of that stuff every day. Every day? Yes, I create something every day. I'm also thinking about investing every single day. It's the only way to do it. Nothing comes for free.

What about health goals? Instead of focusing on how many pounds of muscles I add, I focus on getting at least three strength training workouts a week. And those workouts need to be great. No one ever got stronger by half-assing it.

But I didn't have this mindset all of my life. In fact, I was more of a "good-enough" person until several years ago. I would set goals and hardly ever follow through. But at some point, I realized that's not the way I want to live. It's that simple. No big life-changing event or something dramatic. How about you? Are you satisfied with your days when you're in bed every night? If your answer is no, what are you going to do about that? You can set goals that will help you to change your behavior. Everything is in your hands now. You don't depend on anyone for the outcomes. Simply focus on what you control and think about the actions you need to take every single day of your life. The funny thing is that the less you obsess about the outcomes, the easier things will come to you. When you only focus on the process, you know you're doing it right. It's just like the illustration at the top. Set a goal, turn your back on it, and start working.

Don't be surprised when, one day, you go beyond your goal. Just keep rowing, my friend.

LETTER 42:
ON THE JOY OF SEEING
PEOPLE SUCCEED

In one of the letters that the Stoic philosopher Seneca wrote to his friend, Lucilius, you can sense he was really proud of the progress Lucilius had made. Remember, Seneca started writing letters to Lucilius at a later stage of his life. By that time, he had withdrawn from the busy life of Rome—and his biggest successes were behind him in business and politics.

But Lucilius was in the midst of his career and he was trying to make something of his life. Ancient Rome was bustling with activity and there was always something to do. And also like today, people experienced jealousy. Isn't that a feeling that's as old as humanity? Many of us assume that it's normal to feel jealous. Not the Stoics, though.

Seneca was actually pleased to see Lucilius make progress. He wrote: "I grow stronger and more triumphant and rally in energy, casting off my old age, whenever I realize from your actions and writings how much you have projected yourself beyond yourself—for you long since left the crowd behind you."

Seneca wrote that he grew stronger because he saw his friend succeed. This is a stark contrast with how most people look at others, even their friends and family.

Look, how often do you feel jealous? Maybe your sibling got a promotion and the family can't stop talking about it at the dinner table. Or your best friend started a YouTube channel that took off overnight. Maybe your co-worker was promoted and is now your manager. There are so many things that can make us feel jealous. And what do we do? We start feeling a range of negative emotions, which lead to unhappiness and suffering. We either feel like we're not good enough, or that other people are better. Or we feel anger towards others: "Why that person and not me?"

Everyone knows that jealousy is not a helpful emotion. But in my experience, no one has a good way to overcome feeling jealous except for the Stoics. How Seneca responded to his friend is truly the best way to look at other people's success. When you see other people succeed, use it as inspiration. Just like Seneca, extract energy from other people who do well.

This is the most brilliant strategy because it plays into human nature. What do we care about the most in this world? Sure, we love to say it's the well-being of the planet and so forth. The truth is that many of us mostly care about ourselves and our offspring. When you say,

"I grow stronger when I see other people succeed," what are you actually saying? You're saying that you are benefiting from someone else's success. It's one of the most underrated and overlooked lessons of Stoicism. The Stoics were masters at using trivial circumstances to their benefit. They actually found a way to use situations that would make other people jealous to improve themselves. Any non-Stoic who would guide their friend would at some point feel jealous. "Look at this guy, I'm helping him and he's now more successful than I ever was." It's a scenario that often happens in the workforce.

When I started working at a major IT research firm many years ago, I was assigned a mentor. The guy, his name was Sander, helped me a lot. And with all the support I received, I performed well at my job. At some point, I received more recognition and praise than Sander. From that point, our relationship totally transformed and he even tried to sabotage me less than a year after he helped me. He couldn't stand that I made progress and threatened to overtake him.

But the truth was he was a very knowledgeable person who I learned a lot from. Regardless, it destroyed our relationship. At the same time, I also had another team member, Andre, who was a very experienced, generous, and kind person. I spent a lot of time with him and learned many lessons about business, office politics, and persuasion from Andre. The funny thing is that everyone liked Andre and a lot of folks disliked Sander. So one of my co-workers was super competitive and wanted to be successful at all costs. And the other celebrated other people's success and was very generous with his knowledge. As a result, Andre actually was more successful.

By celebrating other people's success like it's your own, you grow stronger.

You can use it as inspiration and energy to keep moving forward. It's truly a beautiful way to live because everyone gets to win. That's one of the reasons I always wish you the best. So, as always: All the best!

BUILDING WEALTH

"Wise people are in want of nothing, and yet need
many things. On the other hand, nothing is needed by
fools, for they do not understand how to use anything,
but are in want of everything."

— Chrysippus of Soli

LETTER 43:
ON GETTING RICH

When I mention to people that I follow Stoic principles in my life, they often assume I live very frugally and have no desire to grow. I don't know why people have that perception. I think Stoicism and trying to improve your life and career can go hand in hand.

Epictetus, who always advocated a very simple lifestyle in his teachings, said this about money: "If you can make money remaining honest, trustworthy, and dignified, by all means; do it. But you don't have to make money if you have to compromise your integrity."

You see? We can do both. The thing about our society is that we often feel like it's all or nothing. You either live frugally and save, or you chase money and squander it on your desires. And I get it. We always read and hear about extreme cases. On Netflix, we either see documentaries that talk about how greed leads to destruction. Or, we see stuff about how you should give up all your possessions and live a minimalistic lifestyle.

All of these extreme cases give us the idea that there's no middle ground. To me, that's where Stoicism comes in. It's all about living with freedom and peace of mind. As Epictetus said, if you want to make money; do it! But your peace of mind should never depend on money. And that's exactly what Seneca did. He was a very wealthy man in Ancient Rome. He was also politically involved. And he was also a great philosopher. How can that be? Seneca was a Stoic philosopher who also tried to get rich and succeeded? Yes, but he never measured himself by his money. Here's what Seneca said about that: "If you want to weigh yourself up, set aside your money, your house, your rank, and consider your inner man: for as it is, you are entrusting to others the gauge of your quality."

If you can only get rich by giving up your values, don't do it. The key is to be able to look at your life without your money and possessions, and ask yourself: Am I proud of myself?

If we set aside all the external things and figure out that we have, or have done, nothing we're proud of, we have a problem. So no matter what you do, always value your character and values above anything else. That's the Stoic way to approach wealth. What's important is that money has no hold over you. Most people are either afraid of losing their money, or they fear that they will never have enough. Whether you're saving your money or chasing after more, if you're always thinking about money, your life is dominated by it. That's a big price to pay. At the end of the day, money is a tool. Sure, it's great to have more.

As someone who grew up in a family that lived from paycheck to paycheck, I know how painful not having enough money can be. That pain often remains in us for generations. My great-grandfather passed his thriftiness to his son, then he passed it on to his children, but fortunately, not to my mother. While all her siblings are always talking about how expensive everything is, my mom never hesitates to spend money on the "expensive" stuff she values like Chanel perfume or buying groceries without ever looking at the prices. "As long as I can buy these things, I will." That's what she says. To me, this shows that she is actually less fixated on money than her more frugal siblings.

She's less attached to the idea of wealth, which suggests that should she lose some of her wealth, she could deal with it more resiliently.

She knows she wasn't in that position for the majority of her life, and that she might not always be in the future. We need to remind ourselves that we're not around on this planet forever. Life's too short to let money dictate our lives to an extreme. If you want to get rich, go for it. And if you don't, that's fine too. The key is not to get too attached to the outcomes or to link your self-worth to whatever external trappings your life has at any given moment. Whichever way you go, recognize that money is not everything; but your values and character are.

LETTER 44:
ON THE DEADLY PURSUIT
OF MONEY

Do you feel the pressure to earn more? You're not alone. Most of us pursue money. Some do it for the status and so they can buy more expensive things. Others do it so they can travel. There are also many people like me who grew up with little and are dead-set on never being poor again. It really doesn't matter what the reason for pursuing money is. We're all after money in some shape or form.

The rich person can't get enough, the poor person doesn't have enough. Many things in life are not fair. But pursuing money is not necessarily a bad thing as long as you do it in an honest way. Epictetus once said, "If you can make money remaining honest, trustworthy, and dignified, by all means do it."

The Stoic point of view is this:

- Money is important
- We need it to be a member of society

- Providing value to our community is a good thing
- And it generally results in earning money
- But you can't be useful to your community if you're "shameless and corrupt," as Epictetus said
- That's why there are other important things in life
- Things like trustworthiness, integrity, and protecting your values

Look, we can't say that our values are more important than money. Why are people so obsessed with ranking things? In relationships, people often say things like, "Your friends are more important than me."

That's not how I look at life. There are things that are important. And there are things that are not important. I make sure I always value the important over the unimportant.

Making money? Important. Being honest? Also important. That means: Earn an honest living and treat people you interact with well.

Here's another example. My partner? Important. My family? Also important. That means: Spending time with both, communicating openly, and appreciating everyone.

There's no need to rank things in life. You can give equal importance to more than one thing. When you don't, you end up prioritizing only one thing. Think of all the people who blindly chase money and sacrifice their relationships, integrity, and personal values. The legendary investor Warren Buffett once said, "It takes 20 years to build a reputation and five minutes to ruin it."

How true is that? When you screw people they will never trust you anymore. Open up the Wall Street Journal and you'll probably read about another story of how a CEO laid off people over Zoom or how a hedge fund manager blew up a multi-billion dollar fund. This is what I call the deadly pursuit of money.

When you throw away your character and reputation for the chance of earning a few bucks, you're playing with fire. It's really not worth it. When you lose yourself, you're exactly that: Lost. No sane person would sacrifice their happiness for more money. The same is true for your relationships. Some people think that if they become rich, their family and friends will benefit somehow. Well, that might be true in your mind, but not in real life.

"A good friend would rather you didn't compromise your integrity than wish you gave him money," Epictetus wisely said.

You can think about it as much as you want. But you can never say, "Money is the most important thing," because there is no such thing. Money matters. But there are also a lot of other things that matter. Simply prioritize all those important things. And if you don't get rich and stay normal? At least you'll have your values and character. That's far from normal in today's world.

LETTER 45:
ON THE BEAUTY OF A
"NORMAL" LIFE

Last week, I was watching TV with my mom, and we were indulging in a little venting about the pace of the vaccine rollout. "If they keep up this pace, we'll have our vaccine by 2030," we joked.

When we finished our commentary on the news, I changed channels to a show about a Bitcoin millionaire. It was about a guy in his twenties who bought Bitcoin for around $300 apiece (it's around $40K right now). He apparently bought a bunch of them and has been living the lifestyle of the rich and the famous.

My mom has no idea what Bitcoin is, so she asked me how this guy got rich. I explained that it's a digital currency and that this guy saw the opportunity before the mainstream caught on. She responded, "Where can I get some Bitcoin?"

We laughed. But after that, we talked about how good it is to work for your money. It's really hard to see that we're actually blessed with what we have. Good health, somewhat sane family members, a few good friends, and co-workers, having a job—it's a blessing to have a "normal," balanced life.

Seneca often talked about the bliss of moderation. He said: "It is the mark of a great spirit to hold great things in contempt and prefer moderate circumstances over excess; for moderation is useful and life-enhancing, whereas excess harms by its abundance."

Look at life this way. Let's say you have land and you're growing crops. Excessive fertilizer will not make the crops grow any faster. In fact, ask a bunch of farmers, and they will probably tell you that too much fertilizer will only weigh down a crop. Excess is actually harmful. This is not something you often hear in our society.

We celebrate success, fame, and recognition, and we always assume more is better (of all of it). But not having those things is not that bad either.

In many ways, a "normal" life without excess is actually more beautiful. Nothing builds more character than life itself.

I'm a big Jay-Z fan, and one of the things I love most about him is that he got into the entertainment business when he was already his own man. He released his first album when he was almost 27 years old. What's even better is that he had the resources to do it by himself.

In today's rap game, starting at 27 means you're a dinosaur. Take Youngboy NBA, a 21-year-old rapper from Baton Rouge. I like his music too. The guy has already released four albums and SEVENTEEN mixtapes. He also has seven kids and had more legal issues than Jay-Z had in his 51 years on this planet.

One is not better than the other. But what I learned from JayZ is that character matters more than success. You can have all the money and fame in the world, but if you're not a complete human being, what's it good for?

A life of excess only leads to more excess.

We all know how that ends. But somehow, we look at our own lives and compare them to others and think, "I suck." No, screw that. You know how those Reddit traders took on the hedge funds that shorted Gamestop? Well, in our own lives, we're often those hedge funds. We sell ourselves short. Isn't that stupid? Do the opposite: Bet on yourself no matter what the outcome is.

Your life is good when you work on yourself—not when you get recognition. Hard times will define you. But you have to embrace the struggle and become friends with yourself. Accept who you are and own it. Never allow the desire for success to define you. That won't make you a better person. What will? Aim for being a person your best friend always can rely on. Someone who walks through life with a straight back does what they say, and is comfortable in their own skin.

LETTER 46:
ON THE PSYCHOLOGY
OF MONEY

Out of all the Stoic philosophers I've read, Seneca is the one who spoke most about wealth. After all, he came from a wealthy family and didn't have to worry about money for most of his life. He also was Rome's leading intellectual and was the closest advisor of the emperor Nero (who reigned between 54 AD and 62 AD).

But Seneca didn't have status and wealth for his entire life. The last part of his life was tragic. After he lost his influence in politics, he retreated from active life until 65 AD, when he was accused of being part of a conspiracy to murder Nero. As a punishment, Seneca was ordered to commit suicide, which he actually did without resistance. During those last three years of his life, Seneca wrote his best philosophical work. It was a period defined by simplicity and travel. He wrote:

"The man who needs wealth is afraid of it,
and no man enjoys an asset that is a source of
trouble. He is eager to add something to it,
and while he is concentrating on the
increase he has forgotten to use it."

When you believe that being rich is so important that your life depends on it, you will probably do everything to acquire more money. People who think that more money means more happiness usually try their best to make more money. This is the psychology of many people for centuries. The only goal they have is to accumulate more. And in the pursuit of money, those people actually forget why they pursued money in the first place. A great book about money and investing is *The Psychology of Money* by Morgan Housel, a long-time financial writer, and investor. I highly recommend that book to anyone who wants to have a healthy relationship with money and doesn't want to fall for the trap of accumulating more for the sake of accumulation.

As Morgan writes, money is an emotional subject:

"Few people make financial decisions purely
with a spreadsheet." We all like to believe
we're highly rational and analytical people who
don't succumb to common money mistakes.
But we're human beings! Not robots.

And because money is what the world revolves around, it's easy to get caught up in unhealthy behavior. It's healthy to make money a priority and to provide for yourself and your family. It's unhealthy to sacrifice your life and your family just so you can get rich.

As we've seen from Seneca's quote, the problem of unhealthy money behavior is not a new problem. They dealt with the same problems 2000 years ago, and probably from the moment money became important in society around 600 BC.

In my experience, Stoicism provides a great mental model for dealing with money. Just like you shouldn't get attached to your emotions, you shouldn't get attached to the pursuit of wealth. Always remind yourself that you acquire money for a reason, and that reason is primarily to function in society. The Stoics didn't think being very rich determined a person's happiness. What's all that money good for when you don't enjoy your life? Or when you miss important events in your family's life? We and the people we love all are going to die. It might sound morbid, but it's really a good thing to remind ourselves.

Seneca regularly meditated on the loss of money. Sometimes he spent entire days pretending he had no money. He would wear old clothes, eat little, and sleep on the ground. He learned that having no money wasn't something he should fear. When you have some money, you're often afraid of losing it. But not the Stoics. They believed we shouldn't get attached to anything, whether it's money, status, objects, a job, and even people. I like

Seneca's method of reminding himself he didn't need to be rich. Imagine that you don't have any money today.

Skip your daily luxuries. Live simply, even if it's for a day or two. It reminds you that simple is not bad.

You will have something that people who are addicted to freedom don't: Real freedom. After all, isn't the true definition of being wealthy not having to worry about money?

LETTER 47:
ON INSPIRING OTHERS

I really enjoy talking about Stoicism with you because it has practical use in daily life. When the stock market was down a while back, I added the same amount of money I add every month without a flinch. I looked at my account, saw I was down thousands of dollars in a day, didn't care, and moved on. I wasn't like this in the past. I would freak out on the slightest market downturn. But now, I try to remember that it's normal, and I'm not afraid of loss because I know it's temporary. And if the whole financial system collapses? So be it. I'll have other things to work on if a catastrophe like that happens.

When philosophy is so powerful that it changes your life, you want to talk about it with others.

The other day I was having dinner with several members of my extended family. The dinner-time conversation was mostly about negative things: Covid, new variants, crime, inflation, social media, mental health problems, you name it. I didn't say much. But at some point, I said, "Why do you guys talk so much about things you don't control?" No answer. The conversation simply circled back to politics, which is basically where most conversations end up these days. I stopped myself right there.

I used to think that it was my job to tell others about Stoicism because it's such a helpful philosophy. But that's not what the Stoics did. In fact, they didn't talk about Stoicism with people who didn't care about the philosophy. Instead, they practiced what they preached, and kept to themselves. As Epictetus once said: "Sheep don't bring their owners grass to show how much they ate. Instead, they digest it and produce milk and wool. Similarly, don't make a show of principles you live by. Instead, live by them fully and show others by your actions how much you have learned and made it your own."

When we try to tell people about Stoicism and about how they shouldn't waste their time on things they don't control, we're actually making a show of our principles. We're saying: "Look at me, I found the answer to life! Just do this and everything will be better." At least, this is how most people perceive it. But it doesn't matter how people look at it.

What matters is that we live according to our principles. The reason Epictetus said we shouldn't make a show of the principles we live by is that most people interpret it the wrong way when you try to help. You might think, "I want to help this person by passing on ancient advice for living better," while the recipient thinks, "Why is this person telling me this? I'm not stupid! This person is just trying to show off."

The best way to inspire others is by being a good person and performing your duties in life no matter what happens.

Every day, we wake up and do the things we have to do simply because that's our mission. Not because we need to prove to others we're living according to certain principles. What you'll find is that some people will come to you and ask about how you do it.

When others are interested in your ideas or advice, be generous and share as much as you want. The world will only be better if more of us share what we've learned. And the more you practice what you believe in, the more credible you will be. All of that without showing off!

MANAGING YOUR CAREER

"If you accomplish something good with hard work, the labor passes quickly, but the good endures; if you do something shameful in pursuit of pleasure, the pleasure passes quickly, but the shame endures."

— Musonius Rufus

LETTER 48:
ON RESTING VS WORKING

I took a few days off last week because I wanted to rest. It's something I learned from Dale Carnegie. He writes in *How to Stop Worrying and Start Living*, "Rest before you are tired." It's a great piece of advice for avoiding burnout. But for most of my career, I used to wait to take a break until I was already tired and running on fumes. It's like drinking water when you're thirsty. The way to avoid thirst is to stay hydrated. It's the same thing when it comes to resting your body. When you're getting signals from your body that you need rest, it's important to listen.

What are some of those signals? I bet you know it, you probably just ignore it like most of us. Frequent headaches, heavy eyes, sleeping badly, waking up several times in the night, not being able to focus during the day, getting agitated quickly—the usual traits of a person who's behaving irritably. I've trained myself to recognize those signals, and when I see even just some of that stuff, I take a break from most of my goals and work and rest. So I took a few days off last week.

Work is important but being healthy and energized matters more.

It's in no one's interest to beat yourself up until a point you can't function. That's why everyone needs their rest. But sometimes, a short rest is not going to solve it. Sometimes resting can turn into a lifestyle of sloth. When you always are looking forward to resting, it makes you lazy. This is not something we like to hear, but it's the truth. I've been there. It used to be that after every single day of work, I couldn't wait to rest on the couch and watch another episode of my favorite tv show. By Wednesday, I was already looking forward to the weekend so I could rest.

Seneca, who was a proponent of a calm lifestyle, was also against too much rest. He said: "Sometimes rest itself is restless. This is why we must be roused to action and kept busy by the performance of skilled arts whenever this sloth which cannot bear itself puts us in a bad state."

What type of life is that? I was trying to find relief in rest. I was avoiding work. The truth was that I didn't enjoy my career at the time. And that was causing a lot of stress, so I didn't sleep well. Seneca talked about why that happens: "There is no calm repose except when reason has settled it; night causes disturbance, rather than removes it, and merely changes our worries. In fact the dreams of sleepers are as troublesome as their days. The real calm is when a good state of mind unfolds."

When you're chronically worried and your entire life is filled with worry, sometimes the answer is not just to rest, but to find a way to stop worrying. If there's something in your life that's causing chronic stress, either change it or accept it. There is no use in letting it negatively impact your health.

But if you've been working a lot and you're getting agitated, taking a short break will charge your body and mind. You will be excited to get back to work again, which is the default state of mind of a healthy person. If you find pleasure in your work, you won't yearn for rest all the time—only when you actually need it.

LETTER 49:
ON DOING WHAT LIFE
EXPECTS OF YOU

Growing up, I often heard stuff like, "You can be anything you want!" And that motivated me to do well in school, to take care of my body, and to dedicate time and energy to building a career. The idea that you and I can do anything we want is very inspiring, but it's also false.

Another thing I often heard was, "You're the director of your own movie!" That's supposed to motivate you to take matters into your own hands, to be the maker of your own life. While there's some wisdom in that, the Stoic philosopher Epictetus had a slightly different perspective on what life actually is. He said:

"Consider yourself as an actor in a play. The nature of the play—whether short or long—is for the director to decide. The director will also decide whether your role is one of a poor person, a rich person, a cripple, a king, or a commoner.

> You as an actor do not decide these things. Like
> an accomplished actor you need to perform
> the role assigned to you in life skillfully. The
> responsibility for deciding what role you
> play rests with someone else."

The first time I read that, I found it a bit sad. I thought every person was the director of the play, and also the actor. But we need to see things for what they are.

There are some things in life that are handed to us, and we can't change those things.

I always appreciate the humility of Warren Buffett when he's asked about how he became the most successful investor of all time. He argues that a big part of success is winning the "ovarian lottery." He recognizes that he was lucky to be born as a white male in the United States, during a time the founder of Value Investing, Benjamin Graham, lived. At a Berkshire Hathaway's annual shareholder meeting that he holds with his business partner, Charlie Munger, he talked about how lucky they both were: "When we were born the odds were over 30-to-1 against being born in the United States, you know? Just winning that portion of the lottery, enormous plus."

Buffett is obviously being very humble. The man is an absolute genius. But would he be the same if he was born in another country in a different era? He would probably do well, but he wouldn't be the greatest investor of all time. This is a hard thing to accept.

But in today's society, we believe everything is limitless, including our own potential. We see people on social media living luxurious lives. At our jobs, we see people who are younger and less experienced getting promoted. And when we go home, our partners or parents wonder, "Why are you not the CEO by now?"

While we often think we're being encouraging or hopeful when we tell ourselves and others that we can do anything we want, we also have our limitations. Sometimes the odds are stacked against us. Not everyone will reach the top of a company, sport, or social hierarchy. That's the nature of life. And there's nothing wrong with that.

But we collectively ignore the facts of life. The problem is that we live in a constant state of dissatisfaction. The way I see it, the unhappiness of the developed world comes from this phenomenon.

It's not that our lives are bad; we just think our lives are bad and expect that could or should be limitless and extraordinary.

"I should be a millionaire world champion with five hundred thousand followers on social media." Wake up, my friend. That's not real life. As both Epictetus and Buffett pointed out, there are certain things outside of our control. The good thing about living in the 21st century is that we have the opportunity to improve our life situation. That wasn't true in Epictetus' time. When you were born poor, you would stay poor. That's no longer true.

But the truth of the ovarian lottery will never change. Where you're born, what year, your family's socioeconomic status, your physical shape, what your natural talents are, and so forth; that's all written the day you came to this earth. But we can still make the best of what's given to us. We can see ourselves as actors in a play. And we play that role the best way we can.

LETTER 50:
ON BEING YOUR OWN WITNESS

Over the past year, most of us have been working from home and spending more time than usual on our own. Throughout the day, there's no one who's watching what we're doing. It's been the perfect self-awareness exercise to figure out what our true motives are.

So often, we're motivated by getting the approval of other people. The jobs we take, the books we read, the clothes we buy, the pictures we take for social media, the people we associate with. We do those things because we want to be liked by others.

I can't lie, I've lived the majority of my life that way. I only stopped looking for outside approval once I started applying Stoicism to my life. Reading Seneca, Marcus Aurelius, and Epictetus has reminded me that life is not about how people perceive you. It's all about what you think of yourself. At the end of the day, you'll spend the most time with that voice in your head. That's why it's important to actually like yourself. This might sound weird, but do you enjoy spending time alone? Even if it's a few minutes. Or are you always thinking about what other people are doing? Or what so-and-so said about you yesterday? Or, as I often did, thinking about how you somehow can get ahead in life?

When you're always thinking about external things, you risk living your life just to please others. When we do that, we lose our character. Epictetus said it best: "You compromise your integrity when you seek outside approval. Be satisfied that you live up to your rational principles. Be your own witness if you need one. You don't need any more witness than that."

I can relate to that a lot. As kids, we're all conditioned to please others. We get good grades so our teachers and parents will say, "Good job!" And in fact, we need people's approval as kids, otherwise, we can never finish school. The sad thing is that this conditioning remains alive in most adults.

We feel like everything is about approval. In our intimate relationships, we want to make our partner happy. In our careers, we want to make our boss and co-workers happy. In our businesses, we want to please our customers. All of that is great. But it should never be the primary reason we do something. In a relationship, we should enjoy spending time with our partners. At our job, we should be pleased with the job we do. In our business, we should be proud of the products and services we offer.

Whether there's a witness or not, we should still do what we do. I wasn't like that at all in the past. When I played basketball in high school, I would show up at 3:59 pm when our practice was at 4 pm. And I would never work out on my off days.

And when I had a corporate job, I would work harder when I was surrounded by my teammates and boss. When my boss was off, I would slack off more. And in the evenings and weekends, I didn't care much about my work. My witnesses were external. Looking back, it wasn't fair to my teammates, coach, boss, and even to myself. When you're not self-motivated, you never perform at your best.

What do you do when no one's watching? Your actions during those moments define you. Do you work because it matters to you? Do you show up early because you're excited to practice? Do you read books because you want to learn? Do you think of your partner because you care about them? When you're giving everything your best when no one's watching, you know that you're the only witness you need. That's the epitome of self-motivation.

We often look at others for motivation, but we should look within.

By changing your mindset, and becoming your own witness, you never need other people to motivate you. You're always there to keep yourself accountable.

LETTER 51:
ON BEING PRECISE WITH YOUR WORDS

Have you noticed how easy it is to talk and how hard it is to write? Somehow, we put more effort into being precise when we write. We try to be as clear as possible. But when we speak, we tend to go on and on without saying much. Sometimes during conversations with others, I catch myself starting a sentence without awareness of what I actually want to say. That's simply talking for the sake of talking. Even when we talk without awareness, we tend to say things that make no sense or are not precise.

For example, many of us make judgmental observations. Epictetus explained this point well: "If someone bathes quickly, don't say he doesn't bathe properly, say he bathes quickly. If someone drinks a lot, don't say he is a drunk, say he drinks a lot. Unless you know the reasons for their actions how can you be sure of your negative judgment of them? Not judging others too quickly will save you from misperceiving their actions."

This happens all the time these days, especially on the internet. Someone doesn't like X, therefore the person is a Y. The Y is always a label that people use. Someone is a hater, denier, sheep, extremist, gullible, and so forth. Every time people make these types of observations, it means they are making bad observations. But that doesn't mean people are bad or imprecise thinkers. We can only say they are making imprecise observations.

One of the foundational ideas in Stoicism is that we don't know what people think, hence, we should avoid making assumptions about why people do certain things. And yet, this is the favorite pastime of many people. We love to speculate about why people do or say things. That means we rely on assumptions and made-up stories—not on facts. If there's something less precise than that, I'd love to know.

To live like a Stoic, practice precision in your words.

You can start practicing with writing. When you write, you have more time to think about what you say. When you write a sentence, you can take a few seconds to think about it, hit backspace, and start fresh. You can't do that in conversations. One harsh fact about people is that when you say something to them, it's hard to forget. When you're in a heated argument and you call someone names, they feel hurt. You can't hit backspace on that. We often say, "I didn't mean it that way!" Being precise in your words goes beyond avoiding assumptions. It also means you say what you mean. And that you use your words to communicate properly.

Before I started studying and applying Stoicism, I have to admit I didn't pay attention to being precise in the way I communicated. I would just blurt out the first thing that I popped up in my mind. Most of the time that doesn't lead to issues. But when you have important conversations, it can cause problems. For example, if you're having an argument with your spouse, and things get emotional, saying the wrong thing can make everything worse.

If you say something like, "Maybe we should split up," you can't just take it back a few seconds later.

Or if you're having a conversation with a business partner and you say, "I don't know if this will succeed." You might think you're being thoughtful, the other person might think you lack self-confidence.

I like to write a lot because it forces me to be clear, which also translates into the preciseness of my words when I talk. Every time you write something important, take the time to edit your writing several times for clarity. When you write and speak with clarity, you automatically become a good communicator.

Think of all the benefits that Stoicism has. It will not only help you to deal with your emotions. It also helps you to improve your relationships with others through effective communication. Without Stoicism, I wouldn't be writing this letter either. Isn't that fascinating? And it all started with reading the precise words of Seneca, Epictetus, and Marcus Aurelius.

LETTER 52:
ON THE COUNTER INTUITIVE POWER OF DOING LESS

The other day, I was talking to a friend who works out a lot. He said he injured his knee and couldn't exercise his lower body much. I asked how it happened, and he said, "I just took on too much." He was running several times a week, going to boxing class twice a week, and he also lifted weights a few times a week. When you take on more than your body can handle, you inevitably get injured if you don't also take care to recover like a professional athlete.

So many of us have this internal voice that says, "Do more!" Whether that's doing more fun things on the weekend, or taking on more at work, we often have the tendency to do more because we think that's somehow better. That's how we end up living overly busy lives, full of "more."

More goals, tasks, projects, money, vacations, clothes, experiences, exercise, and so forth. There are many times I get excited about my work and feel good. And because I enjoy working and being active, I do a lot. I might write a lot, record podcasts, create new videos, take on more work at my family business, and also do more fun things like travel. My mindset during those times is: "Nothing is enough. I can do more of everything."

But those moments are never long-lasting, right? It's like you're in this crazy sugar rush. You're like a six-year-old who ate a bag of Skittles and only wants to go, go, go. But after some time, you crash hard. The post-sugar-high-crash is pretty bad because you feel so drained you only want to sleep. And if you keep living your life from one high to the other, you never have any real peace. Or, like my friend with the busted knee, you end up injuring yourself.

But we don't want to live from injury to the other, with some healthy bouts in-between.

You get injured, recover, get agitated because you couldn't work out, pick things up again, go hard until you get injured again. And so the cycle repeats itself. There's a better way of living. As the philosopher-king Marcus Aurelius once wrote: "If you seek tranquility, do less." It's counterintuitive because so often our innate drive is to do more, and because more so often seems to signify "better." But when we do less, we can be more consistent. We can pay attention to the things that really matter to us.

Aurelius continued: "do what's essential—what the logos of a social being requires, and in a requisite way. Which brings a double satisfaction: to do less, better. Because most of what we say and do is not essential. If you can eliminate it, you'll have more time and more tranquility. Ask yourself at every moment, 'Is this necessary?' We need to eliminate unnecessary assumptions as well." I like to think about that question often. In fact, you can do it with me. Ask:

"What's something I'm doing that I can easily do without?"

Maybe it's a side project that is only making you frustrated. Maybe it's going out with co-workers every single Friday. It could be anything. Say no, at least for now. You can always decide to pick something up again. The goal is to clear your mind of any excess clutter. Focus on what's important.

LETTER 53:
ON FINISHING WHAT YOU START

In life, sometimes it's more important that you see your plans through until the end than to have the perfect plan. I remember when I was in my first year of college and so many of my classmates were doubting themselves. We studied business administration, and many weren't sure whether the degree would be exactly what they needed.

My friends would constantly look at other degrees and compare. "What if I should get a different degree?" I did none of that. Back then, I also had no clue what I wanted to do after I graduated. I knew one thing: I had made a decision and I was committed to sticking with it until the end. It was just four years. I knew that I didn't want to be in a specialized field, so I didn't worry about whether my degree was perfect. I focused on studying, enjoying my time at college, and making sure I finished my degree within four years.

Out of the people I knew who quit the degree, most became chronic quitters. One of them truly was in the wrong place. He ended up becoming a physiotherapist. Sometimes, you make the wrong plan and start going in the wrong direction, and you really do need to course-correct.

We need to be self-aware enough to realize whether we want to quit because something is hard or are on the wrong path.

Too often, we put too much weight on our decisions, which causes anxiety and overwhelm.

The reality is that many things are not permanent. You can get a degree in business and end up working in art. You can have a job at a restaurant, and end up as an investor. Life is long. Sometimes we pursue things that don't work out. But as long as you focus on seeing things through, you become stronger and smarter.

If you do what you say, you become reliable.

This is something the Stoics often talked about. To them, living according to Stoic values mattered more than what you did. How you do things is what matters. Here's what Epictetus said: "Once you undertake to do something, stick with it and treat it as something that should be carried through. Don't pay attention to what people say. It should not influence you in any way."

Once we set our minds to doing something, we will not only have to deal with our own inner resistance but as Epictetus said, with what people say. "Are you sure this is the right thing?" That's something people often ask us when we want to do something new, whether that's picking a career, starting a business, getting married, pursuing a degree, traveling the world, you name it. When asked, "Are you sure?", many of us start doubting ourselves. Maybe the person asking the question wants to help you to think things through, or maybe they purposefully want you to doubt yourself so you don't take action. It doesn't matter whether people have good or bad intentions.

What matters is that you don't let people influence you. If you want to do something and you know it's the right thing to do, go for it. Finish what you start. As long as we're not harming others (or ourselves), we can pursue anything we want. Just make sure you carry through your plans. When you do that consistently, you can truly rely on yourself. After all, you know that you will do what you say. You can trust yourself.

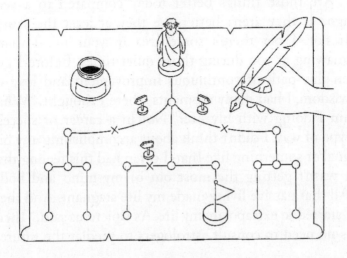

LETTER 54:
ON SHAPING YOUR FUTURE

How do you feel about your life right now? Forget about everything that's going on in the world. Look at the personal things that matter to you. For most of us, it's our character, consistency, happiness, health, those kinds of things. The things that we have power over.

Are those things better today compared to a year ago? If they aren't better, are they at least the same? If not, I bet there's some area in your mind that's gnawing at you during those quiet times. Before I got on this path of continuous improvement and love of wisdom, I had many moments where I thought, "What am I doing with my life?" Not in a career or success type of way. I didn't think about accomplishing any big goal or something like that. I often had this feeling that I wasn't getting the most out of my mind and body. All that passive living made my life stagnant. And then I started to extrapolate my life. As Epictetus said, "There is no need to consult astrologers to predict the future."

You can simply look at your actions today and look at the common results you get.

- If you never learn new things, you won't be any smarter in a year
- If you never challenge yourself physically, you won't be any stronger in a year

These are the only things that are within our control. That's why worrying about things like the economy or geopolitics is fruitless. Epictetus said the overall future of the world is not something we control, and therefore it should be "nothing to us."

However, our actions should be everything to us. By changing your actions today, you can shape your tomorrow. Here's what I did to make that change. I started to read two books a week for three years. I started to lift weights and run consistently. I started writing books and creating courses. I didn't focus on external goals like how much money I earned or whether I had the perfect beach body.

When you do things that improve yourself, it's only a matter of time before your entire life changes. But here's the key if you want to make a change. When you're on your journey, 99 per cent of the time you'll feel like there's no progress.

You just keep going at it. You learn, work at your job, exercise, and you'll probably feel tired at the end of the day. That's the feeling of a good day's work. That's the feeling you should cherish. It's a sign that you're moving forward. Instead of getting frustrated because you're not seeing any big progress from day to day, look at how you feel at the end of the day.

If you can't get to sleep; worrying and feeling bad because your life is stagnant, it's time to make a change. But when you're in bed and you're tired because you squeezed the most out of your day, you're on your path of shaping your future. You're becoming smarter, better, and stronger.

BEING WITH PEOPLE

"It never ceases to amaze me: we all love ourselves more than other people, but care more about their opinion than our own."

— Marcus Aurelius

LETTER 55:
ON THE LIBERATION OF
KEEPING THINGS TO YOURSELF

In The Netherlands, where I grew up, we have this saying that can't quite be translated into English: "Iemand in zijn waarde laten." Loosely translated from the Dutch, it means that you should simply accept people and avoid trying to convince them. But that's not what it actually means. If you translate that sentence word for word, it says: Leave someone in their own worth. The true meaning behind that saying is that you want someone to keep their dignity.

You don't want to attack their beliefs and belittle them because you happen to think differently. The other day, I was talking to one of my neighbors who's self-employed. He installs water treatment systems at companies and people's homes, so he meets many individuals every day. We were talking about the lengthy debates people are having about vaccines at work or in social situations. He used that saying. He said one of his best friends has an opposing view but he just accepts him for who he is.

Out of curiosity, I asked him what he meant by "Iemand in zijn waarde laten" in that specific context. He said that when his friend tries to convince him with all these types of persuasive YouTube videos, he just listens to his friend. And then his friend eventually stops talking about it because he doesn't feed him. My neighbor keeps to himself, even with his best friend who has a different view on certain topics. That's the only way you can stay real friends with people who have opposing views; by not judging each other and letting people keep their dignity.

"If you have chosen a simple life, don't make a show of it. If you want to practice simplicity, do so quietly and for yourself, not for others."

That's one of the things Epictetus taught in his philosophy school in Nicopolis, Ancient Greece. When I discovered philosophy for the first time, I wanted to share it with everyone I knew. It's natural that when you find something that really has a positive impact on your life, you also want the same for others.

Wanting to help people you see struggling is a good instinct. But an important principle of Stoicism is to keep things to yourself and only talk about the philosophy with others who practice it. Seneca would discuss Stoic principles in his letters to his good friend, Lucilius. But he would also say, "Withdraw into yourself, as far as you can. Associate with those who will make a better man of you."

This might sound selfish, but it's actually a very noble thing. The Stoics accepted everyone for who they were. They didn't bother trying to change people's views. It's actually a rather respectful stance. Often, when we try to change someone's point of view, it's because we don't really understand—or haven't even tried to understand—why they think the way they do. Just look at how people who politically lean to the left judge the people who lean to the right, and vice versa.

I wonder what Epictetus would do if he were alive today. Would he have social media? Would he show off his simple life on YouTube? Would he tweet his wisdom? Whatever it would be, I think he would only focus on teaching his ideas to people who actually cared about Stoicism. It's hard to imagine Epictetus posting a picture of himself in his new car or something like that. We will never know what he would do. It also doesn't matter. We know that the Stoics lived for themselves.

If you want to live for yourself, you also want to keep things to yourself as much as you can. There's no need to comment on everything you hear and see. Just let others be.

That's not only the noblest thing you can do, it also gives you more lasting pleasure because you're valuing yourself the most.

LETTER 56:
ON LEARNING FROM PEOPLE'S NEGATIVE BEHAVIOR

Have you noticed how we're often quick to judge others when they behave badly but don't look at ourselves with that same critical eye? I was at a store last week when someone got angry because the store clerk couldn't accept an item the customer wanted to return. I didn't catch what the reason was, but the customer started cursing and asking for the manager. When the manager showed up, the situation got worse because nothing changed about the policy. The customer wanted to return something but didn't get their way.

I'm sure there was a valid reason for refusing the return. Was the aggressive behavior valid? Of course not.

We all have a sense of what's right and wrong when we see it. But not so much when we're in it.

I remember how I once got angry at a bank employee. I applied for a new account at the bank and they called me up and asked me a bunch of questions.

It was their policy, but somehow the person really annoyed me so I started raising my voice and saying that it was bullshit to ask me those questions. We got into a shouting match and I said they should cancel my request. After I hung up, I was angry for the rest of the day. Sometime later, I was reading Marcus Aurelius' *Meditations*, when I stumbled upon a quote that couldn't be more relevant:

"When faced with people's bad behavior, turn around and ask when you have acted like that. When you saw money as a good, or pleasure, or social position. Your anger will subside as soon as you recognize that they acted under compulsion (what else could they do?)."

I love this perspective from Aurelius—who was arguably the most powerful person in the West—because it's so humble. Instead of judging others and labeling them as "bad people," he looks at their behavior and then looks at himself. This is something I really learned from Stoicism. In the past, I would do what most people do: Judge and never look in the mirror. It's really easy to look at someone who displays unacceptable behavior, and then think you're better than them. "Oh look at this guy who's drunk on the plane. What an asshole. Who does that?" I said that to my brother once when we were on a flight, many years ago. Now, I challenge myself to adopt the Marcus Aurelius approach. When you're confronted with bad behavior, see it as an opportunity to avoid judgment. Instead, look inwardly.

Remind yourself of the times you didn't live up to your values. And think about how you can avoid that in the future.

But this doesn't mean we should be pushovers. What if someone confronts us with bad behavior? How do we respond? I like how my mother always approaches people, whether that's at work, the doctor's office, or in a store: Firm and polite. She's assertive and says what she thinks. But at the same time, she doesn't put up with bullshit. It's a difficult approach because most people behave extremely.

Whether it's extremely nice, when you want to avoid confrontation at all costs, or extremely aggressive when it becomes flat-out rude. Somewhere in the middle is the sweet spot. It's a place that requires self-awareness. If you behave badly, you have the ability to be aware of that, and correct yourself. It's a great way to go through life.

LETTER 57:
ON THE TRUE VALUE
OF FRIENDSHIP

Over the last few months, I've been hearing a lot about this new social media app, Clubhouse. It's an app that connects people who want to talk about all kinds of subjects. I tried it last month. And I really don't get why people prefer talking to strangers, when they could use that time to call their friend, sibling, mother, father, or anyone else who's close to them.

Those meaningless conversations on social media will not be there for you when you struggle or feel lonely. Those people are probably also not your real friends. It reminds me of all the empty friendships I've had in the past. In college, my friends were the guys I went to bars with. After that, my friends were the people I spent my weekends with. And when I worked at a corporation, it was the folks I went to TGIF drinks with. But those people were not my real friends.

Here's how Seneca described superficial relationships: "These are what people call friendships of convenience; a man adopted from self-interest will please only as long as he is useful. This is why a crowd of friends surrounds men in times of success but there is a desert around their ruin, and friends flee when they are put to the test."

The first time I realized some friends are not actually your friend was when I went to grad school. At some point, I got tired of the weekly partying and got serious about my education and personal development. I preferred to study or have conversations about life with my friends. But some of my friends back then were not interested in that. So gradually, we grew apart when our common interest—partying—disappeared. I initially thought that was sad. "We spent so much time together and had so many good times, and now we never see each other." That's the nature of life. Through reading the Stoics, I learned that we must accept the change that comes with life. Seasons change, people change, and you change.

There is nothing wrong with that. We need to be okay with that. But sometimes, you grow together. Ten years ago, I became friends with Quincy. At the time, we were both in our early twenties and liked to go out. We were part of a group of six guys who hung out together a lot: We talked every day and saw each other every Saturday night. We often met up at my apartment and would spend the whole evening and night just having fun. Sometimes we went out, sometimes we stayed at the apartment.

Eventually, the other guys went their own way, but Quincy and I remained friends. We always had the most in common. We've gone in different directions in our lives as well, but we always supported each other. And wanted to see the other succeed and be happy. To me, that's what real friendship is about.

Seek out people who have the same values as you. Friendship is not about quantity. Three friends are enough to spend your time with. As Seneca said, most people will not be your friend when they are put to the test.

But that doesn't mean you can't have fun with a co-worker or fellow student. Looking back, I still have a lot of good memories. It's just that most friends come and go, which is not a reason to get sad. I prefer to go deep with people, and really care about the few friends I have. That's the true value of friendship. Not someone you can call to ask for help with moving, or someone to go partying with. No, a friend is someone who thinks and cares about you, even when you don't see or need each other. And whenever you do need each other, you're always there.

LETTER 58:
ON BEING GENTLE
IN YOUR INTERACTIONS

What triggers you? I can be very impatient, which is not Stoic at all. I especially get triggered when I have to wait somewhere. Doesn't matter whether it's in traffic or the line at the supermarket. "C'mon, really? Can this line move any slower!?" Somehow, I have a talent for picking the line that moves the slowest. That shouldn't be a big deal because waiting an extra minute isn't the end of the world.

But if you're impatient, it feels like the biggest issue in the world at that moment. Impatience makes us treat others poorly, and for some weird reason, we often behave the worst toward the people we care about the most. One thing that has helped me to become more patient is an idea I picked up from Epictetus. He said:

"**Always conduct yourself as though you are at a formal dinner. If the dish has not reached you yet, don't be impatient. Wait your turn. When it comes around to you, reach out and take a modest amount.**"

I love this idea of imagining you're at a formal dinner, especially with people you know. You might be hungry and in a hurry to eat, but if you're surrounded by acquaintances, you'll be on your best behavior. It's a gentle and restrained way of interacting with others, but also with yourself. That's something we often forget. When we're triggered, we don't only lash out at others, we also treat ourselves badly. The key is to be more gentle in our inner conversations as well. Epictetus believed we also should be gentle with our wealth. How does that work? Be modest, that's all. If your wealth decreases, don't try to chase it back. That's one of the key strategies of living a peaceful life: Never chase anything too hard.

It's fine to want money, status, love, respect. To some degree, we all want to have those things in our lives. And there's nothing wrong with wanting them. But once these outcomes become our primary goal, everything will go south. You know, Seneca was a wealthy and respectable character in Ancient Rome for most of his life. And the Stoics didn't necessarily despise wealth. They simply could do it with or without it. This mindset made a profound impact on the way I live. I remember chasing everything I wanted in life:

Money, jobs, degrees, friends, lovers. But once I stopped, things came to me more naturally. And if things don't come to me? So what? I don't need much to be happy.

Let me ask you this: Would you rather be rich or poor? Okay, that's an unfair question. Everyone prefers to be rich. But the Stoics didn't mind being poor either. Sounds weird, but it's true.

When you adopt this mindset, you stop chasing things in life. What you'll find is that when you aspire to improve yourself, your relationships, and your skills, the things you want will come to you. That's exactly like being at a formal dinner. You wait your turn, be on your best behavior, and the food will be served.

Be gentle in your interactions with others and with yourself. Don't push yourself to go after your career goals too hard. Avoid thinking you're behind on anything. Stop being in a rush. And if you're acting gently that way, you will be "entitled to dine with the gods" as Epictetus beautifully said.

LETTER 59:
ON ERADICATING ENVY

One of the good things about the pandemic was that we quickly got used to being on our own. It was a forced exercise in self-reliance. When you spend most of your time at home, often the result is that you look at what you want to get out of your days. It's a good way to live because you're focusing on what you control.

But as more and more things got back to normal, we started to look outwardly again. And when we do that, we automatically start comparing ourselves to others. And then, envy creeps into your system. When that happens, we start making stupid decisions. We do things that are out of character. We waste our energy looking at the lives of others. And worst, we think our lives suck compared to others. Don't be fooled by the outward appearance of other people. When people show off their success, possessions, luxurious holidays, and prestige, they are masking something. When you look at what someone is sharing on social media, you always have to remember that you're seeing a curated version of what they want to share.

> Epictetus said it best: "People with more prestige, power, or some other distinction are not necessarily happier because of what they have. There is no reason to be envious or jealous of anyone."

Jealousy is one of the biggest problems in our careers as well. For example, a lot of writers compare themselves to others. They look at external factors: Someone's followers, likes, or people they are friends with. This is nonsense. Why should we compare ourselves with others? It's a losing game because there is always someone "better" than you. If you have one million readers, there's always someone with two million, and someone else with ten million.

Another reason for jealousy is when we see certain people hanging out with each other. We want to be a part of their club. But when you see people name-dropping and spending time with certain people, understand that they may be insecure. They measure themselves by the people who they spend time with. Let me give you an example of how this works in the music industry. When young artists are coming up, they are always concerned with getting "co-signed" by established artists. They want to attach their image to someone who's successful.

One of my favorite rappers, J. Cole, did this when he started. He signed with Jay-Z's record label and had a lot of other famous artists on his first album. But as he came into his own as an artist, he let all of that go. His latest three albums have zero features. It's all him. And he's still one of the most successful rappers in recent history.

But the problem is that most artists never establish their own identity. They always need that co-sign. They want to get close to other successful people because they feel like they are not good enough. And it seems like that's more important than their music.

But as Epictetus says, we should only focus on our freedom: "Our concern should be our freedom, not titles and prestigious positions. The way to freedom is not to be too concerned about things we don't control."

Every time you feel envious, check your priorities. Take envy as a sign to adjust your perspective. And look, it happens to all of us. I'm someone who dislikes social media, but there are times I get caught looking at fancy mansions and luxurious vacations. When that happens, I look at my own house, and it suddenly doesn't seem good enough compared to an eight bedroom villa with a sea view. So I take this as a sign to practice Stoicism.

I go within myself again and focus on what I control. As you can see from these letters, that's always the answer. Whether the problem is jealousy or overthinking, we can always find the solutions within ourselves.

And before I end this letter, I want to share this. It's a good thing to be satisfied with your life the way that it is. I know that the grass is always greener. But if you're healthy and you've got a few people who care about you, life ain't so bad.

LETTER 60:
ON NOT CARING ABOUT
WHAT PEOPLE THINK

The way I see it, you have two options for going about the way you live. You can fit in, taking the path that's been laid out by others. Or, you can create your own path. The former option is the default mode in society. When you're born, your family and the world automatically project their expectations on you. Your parents probably want you to have what they didn't have. In my case, my parents didn't go to college and didn't have white-collar jobs—so they really wanted that for me.

But that's not all you have to deal with. There are many cultural and societal norms we have to comply with, our whole lives. Children go to school, learn how to take orders, do what they are told, get punished when they misbehave, join sports teams, play with their friends, and so forth. Often, the kids who don't perfectly fit into that path get bullied. This is one of the most problematic things about adolescence, and it can mess up the rest of your life. Every kid learns that being different is bad (you get bullied or disciplined) and that as long as you fit in, you will be rewarded.

And what do we do as adults? We do what we're conditioned to do: Fit in. But as we grow up, we see that the people who are successful and happy are usually the ones who don't follow the traditional path. The outsiders, mavericks, odd ones; are the ones who created their own path. They sweated, struggled, and paid the price to do their own thing. And as a result, they are often better off.

The key is that the happy people usually don't care about what others think.

So many of us desperately want to be that person who's carefree and relaxed. You can be that person. Why wouldn't you be able to create your own path?

I was talking to a friend of a friend the other day, and when I said I'm a full-time writer, she said, "That's so cool. I always wanted to write a novel." She works at this fancy marketing consultancy firm now. I asked why she never started writing. You don't have to quit your day job to try something creative. When I started writing, I also had other work. She said, "I'm afraid of what people in my field will say if they find out I wrote a novel. Or what if they read it!?"

We often feel embarrassed just by the thought of doing something. I've met a lot of people who couldn't stand the thought of living a different life than what their family approved of. Just the thought alone. They didn't even take one step. Look, it would be different if you were 18 years old and come home day and say, "Mom and Dad, I'm not going to law school as you guys want. I'm going to become a dolphin trainer in Ecuador." That would be weird, especially because there are probably no dolphins in Ecuador. The point is, there has to be some benefit to being an independent adult: You're in charge.

What's something you're "afraid" of doing? Why even be afraid of what people think? Instead of being afraid, which puts you in a negative state of mind, reframe the thought to: "I'm curious to hear what others think. "There's nothing wrong with asking people you respect for their opinion. I do that all the time. I'm never afraid of their opinions because I don't care if people judge me. As Epictetus once instructed his students: "You do not care if others think you are naïve or stupid. Your only concern is to keep your focus on yourself, so you don't damage your progress."

Don't you love the directness of that quote? You should not care. Period. Decide to be a person like that. You can still be thoughtful and respectful. When you decide to create your own path, be prepared to receive criticism and unsolicited advice. "I would do so and so." I heard that type of stuff when I started writing my first book. Some people raised their eyebrows and said stuff like, "Wow, that's unusual." That's because most people think you need to be qualified to write books. The same people are now surprised I've sold more than 100,000 books online since then. But I never tell those same people about it. What's the point? Like Epictetus said, focus on yourself.

You can decide to do something different in life. If it doesn't work out, so be it.

At least you're not trying to fit in. People who try hard to fit in end up frustrated. They don't know who they are because they've spent their whole lives listening to others. That's the recipe for an identity crisis. You can avoid that fate by not caring about what others think. Just do the right thing and be a good Stoic.

Even if your life is not perfect, it's your life. That's worth more than anything.

LETTER 61:
ON SHARING YOUR JOY
WITH OTHERS

In today's disconnected and individualistic world, it's easy to forget that we're social creatures. But somehow, our modernday lifestyles force people to be more individualistic. It seems like many of us are too busy to spend time building deep, caring, and solid relationships with others.

To me, it's always more important to have deep relationships than a nice house, car, vacation, etc. For what use is anything in the world without the ability to share it with people you love? Seneca, someone who appreciated the importance of friendship, once said that there's no "enjoying the possession of anything valuable unless one has someone to share it with."

It seems like we sometimes forget that when we're too busy living. But no matter how busy we are, we should always make time to maintain our important relationships. While it might seem like the people we know from school, work, sports, and nightlife are good company, they are often not our true friends. Real friends are the people we're most inclined to take for granted. Our own partner/spouse, parents, siblings, and best friends. Those are the people who truly care about us. And those are also the people who will participate in your joy.

Think about what you do when something good happens in your life. What do you usually do first? Probably call someone you can't wait to share it with, right?

- When I got an award at my first job, I called my mother.

- When I bought my first house, I called my best friend.

- When my father secured our first office space, he called me.

- When my brother's short film was accepted into a festival, he called me.

- When my best friend got engaged, he called me.

Every one of these situations revolved around a shared feeling of joy. When you genuinely wish someone the world, you know that's a good relationship. And we don't need to have dozens of those types of relationships. If you have a few people who you know care about you, and you care about them, you're good. When you have someone to share good times with, you also have someone to share the tough times with.

Life isn't always joyful. Sometimes we go through bad times that hurt. But those bad times always hurt less when you have good people in your life.

One good person who's there for you is enough. But you also have to be there for them. And that's the most important thing. When you have someone to share good times with, you also have someone to share the tough times with.

To be a good friend, we should never focus on what the other does. Focus on what you do. Be the friend you want to have. Dedicate time and energy to people who understand. This means you don't want to give someone your time who doesn't appreciate it. When others are not emotionally invested in a relationship, you can tell. Be honest about that.

If others don't want to be in your life, so be it. We should never try to force any type of relationship. Just know that there are many people in the world who do care about deep relationships. It's much better to dedicate your time to finding those people if you don't have them already. Most of us already have a few people with whom we always were close. We just didn't maintain the relationship. We never said stuff like, "I appreciate you."

Look, no matter how cool or badass you are, it's good to let people know you appreciate them. That's all it takes to build relationships: Appreciation.

DEALING WITH HARD TIMES

"Even if some obstacle comes on the scene, its appearance is only to be compared to that of clouds which drift in front of the sun without ever defeating its light."

— Lucius Annaeus Seneca

LETTER 62:
ON LIVING THROUGH
ANXIOUS TIMES

Before the war broke out in Ukraine, many people didn't expect it would actually happen. It reminded me a bit of the early days of Covid. Most people thought it was just like the flu and wouldn't interrupt their lives. Then, everything changed. The problems caused by Covid-like inflation, aggression, fear, not to mention the health problems caused by the illness itself-will linger for years, maybe even decades. Just like The Great Depression in the 1930s. The people who lived through that time kept the scars forever.

Same thing with WWII or any other war. I know this firsthand; my parents experienced war when they lived in Tehran in the 1980s. It was an eight-year war that impacted every aspect of life. That type of experience will be with you forever, even when you live in a safe country. But you can't allow it to take away your passion for life. A great example is the investor Sam Zell, who talks about how his parents fled Poland in 1938. In his book, he mentions that his whole family, who were Jewish, were afraid of antisemitism. But only his father felt a real urgency to get out of Europe. His parents got on the last train out of Poland before the Nazis bombed the train tracks. Zell's family went on a two-year journey to finally reach America, where his father became an entrepreneur.

I can relate to that story because my parents also fled because of a war. And they also started from nothing. During the initial period of war, or when a crisis is going on, you're continuously dealing with danger. Even if you're sitting at home in a safe country now, you still hear about the threat of a nuclear war. If you don't deal with these emotions, it causes anxiety. What I've learned from people who have been through horrible times is that you always must be alert. You must be prepared for anything, ready to do whatever it takes, whether that's keeping calm and carrying on like the Brits during WWII, or fighting like the Ukrainians. We don't know what will happen in the future, or what we'll be called upon to do.

But as Seneca said, "Fortune falls heavily on those for whom she's unexpected. The one always on the lookout easily endures."

When you're not alert, things come to you as a shock. As unexpected. That's the worst way to live. As a Stoic, you want to be alert, but not paranoid. You want to listen, analyze, think, and then act if necessary. You want to look at facts, and not live in fear.

One important aspect of that is interpreting the news. Since there's so much information in the world, it can be really difficult to decide what you should pay attention to, and what you should actually do. My recommendation is to stay away from places like Twitter or forums which are filled with armchair experts who think they know everything about wars, pandemics, politics, power, and dozens of other topics. When you listen to what others say, you're listening to their version of what's going on. You're outsourcing your thinking to others. Here's the recipe for becoming a dependable person: When you face a crisis, and no one is there to help you rely on your own thinking and decision-making. Use the principles of Stoicism to look at what's inside your control, and make use of that power.

My parents were one of the few people in their families who had the courage to leave. That was the only thing inside their control. Sam Zell talked about how almost his entire family perished. They decided to ride out the war and assumed they would be fine. Life is complex and harsh. The Stoics realized that like no one else. They encouraged us to be independent thinkers. And to prepare for whatever. That's the recipe for a virtuous life.

LETTER 63:
ON BEING GRATEFUL FOR
THE LITTLE THINGS

One of my friends said he's committed to seeing his parents more. I asked him why, and he said that he made some calculations. He said, "My parents are in their seventies. We usually see each other twice a year. My grandparents on both sides died around the age of 84. So at that rate, I would probably see my parents only 20 more times in my life."

As a result of a simple calculation, he became more grateful for the moments he spent with his parents, and he tried to see them more often. In our lives, there are so many things we take for granted. Because we humans have this weird trait; we hardly ever regret the things we did. Instead, we regret the things we didn't do. When my grandmother was on her deathbed, she kept going on and on about the things she didn't do. And it wasn't crazy stuff. It was more like; I wish I appreciated my time with certain family members more.

In life, there are many things we can't change. Every day, we get one day closer to death. And instead of being grateful, we worry about things that are minor compared to death.

One of my favorite gratitude exercises comes from Epictetus. He proposed we do the following: "Whenever you face difficult situations in life, remember the prospect of death and other major tragedies that can and do happen to people. You will see that, compared to death, none of the things you face in life is important enough to worry about."

It takes a little while to train yourself to think this way, but I guarantee it works. Compared to death, nothing we worry about or get upset about matters. My friend who calculated the times he will see his parents said he no longer gets frustrated when he talks with them. You know how things often are with family; sometimes we get under each other's skin. We argue we get disappointed, we maybe even call each other names.

But if you make yourself aware of the fact that this is maybe the last time you're seeing the person you love, you'll let all the minor things slide.

Look, this doesn't mean everything is acceptable because, "hey, we're all going to die!" That's too nihilistic. The Stoics used this exercise for small things. Stuff that's just not worth getting upset about. They knew damn well that we risk wasting our time and energy on those insignificant things.

Instead, enjoy the valuable things. For example, the fact that you're alive at this very moment. You're here! You don't even need to see a beautiful sunset or walk through the rain, or any other cheesy thing, to be grateful for life. I bet any person who's on their deathbed would give everything up to have a few extra days of life. Just being alive is the biggest thing one can be grateful for.

LETTER 64:
ON THE UPS AND DOWNS
OF LIFE

I love this quote from Marcus Aurelius about the nature of life: "The world's cycles never change—up and down, from age to age." Let's be honest, do you expect that life should always be good? You do, right? I think most of us grow up that way. We think that life should gradually improve. We hear stories about how the economy and the world have been improving gradually every year for the past decades, and we think that's the normal trajectory for everything in life. Things go up like a linear relation in algebra. If x goes up, y will also go up.

We assume that if we get older, we should automatically get everything together. Then, we actually grow older and figure out that no one knows what they are doing. There's no linear relationship between age and wisdom, or age and wealth. If that were true, every person beyond a certain age would be a rich genius. The truth is that life doesn't go up all the time we're alive. We also experience downs from time to time. Sometimes those downs can take a few days, sometimes months. And if you're unlucky, maybe even years.

A lot of people talk about how bad 2020 was for them just because they had to work from home and couldn't go on vacations. One of my friends had a really shitty 2020. In January of that year, he tore his ACL in a cycling accident, and he got surgery in February. When he was recovering, the coronavirus pandemic broke out, and he couldn't go to physiotherapy, which harmed his recovery. He had to walk on crutches before his surgery, and for weeks after.

Then, around the summertime, he got Covid, which took him out for nearly three weeks. After the summer, he felt better and started doing chores at the house. The poor guy threw his back out and couldn't do anything else but lie in bed for two weeks. He also has young kids; so his wife had to take care of them and him for all the weeks he was out. Almost a year later, he's doing well and has pretty much fully recovered. But it took a year and a half to feel close to what he felt before his knee injury. Last week, he got Covid again. This is stuff we can't control.

As Marcus Aurelius said: "Whether it's atoms or nature, the first thing to be said is this: I am a part of a world controlled by nature. Secondly: that I have a relationship with other, similar parts. And with that in mind, I have no right, as a part, to complain about what is assigned me by the whole."

While I do believe we have a lot of personal freedom and can decide to pursue our own path, we also must recognize there are a lot of things we can't influence.

Sometimes we tend to think we are the true masters of our destiny. We assume that life is like a movie, and we're the writer, director, and actor. That's not a realistic view of life. In reality, we're only the actor. And we're given a role that we need to play. The Stoics believed we need to play that role to the best of our ability. That doesn't mean you need to fit in. No, you can still give the role your own twist. Look at it this way. In the past few decades, several different actors have played the role of Joker in Batman movies. From Jack Nicholson to Jared Leto. My all-time favorite depiction of the Joker is by the late Heath Ledger in The Dark Knight. No one has played it so well than him. And no one other than Heath Ledger could've played that role in that specific way.

In life, we do the same. We decide how we play our roles. We have the power to shape our outlook on life. We all have our unique styles and personalities. We just don't have the power to change most things about life. While that might sound limiting, it's actually liberating when you think about it more deeply. You don't have to waste so much energy getting angry about why life is the way it is. When things are good, simply enjoy. When things are bad, go through it. There's a cyclicality to life that should always give you enough perspective that good times will follow bad times. Here's to both!

LETTER 65:
ON GETTING UNSTUCK

Sometimes one little negative thing can set you on this whole downward spiral. Last week I was talking to my friend Dave about what it feels like to be stuck. Dave was saying that he got a cold a few months ago, which made him stop working out and eating healthy, which made him feel worse. Then, his sleep started suffering from that, which made him tired and unfocused during the day, which ultimately impacted his work.

Haven't we all experienced something like this? One event can cause a ripple that lasts for months. The key is to break the downward spiral because if you don't, you will start hating your life for no good reason. That's what happened recently to another friend I caught up with. He mentioned how the same thing happened to him, but he remained in that negative mindset. "After a while, I started disliking my job for no reason. I just didn't like anything. And at home, I started having more fights with my wife."

We often are not aware of what causes our frustration. We think that the solution to our unhappiness is to change the thing that seems most immediately to be causing it. You might think that your job is making you unhappy, so you look for another one. But all the while, the problem wasn't your job, it was how you felt.

When everything seems to be melancholic in your life, and you're just not excited about anything, try the following: Create a new, meaningful goal. When you stay in your own head, simmering in your own thoughts, the last thing you want to do is focus more on yourself. Start to focus on something outward. Look at something outside yourself, ideally something that impacts others. My friend Dave is an entrepreneur, and he talked about how he decided to do a complete redesign of one of his main products. He received feedback from people who he respected, and that gave him the inspiration to make a few changes so his customers would get a better experience.

Every time I'm stuck or don't have energy, I come up with new things to work on. But I only focus on the things that really fire me up. Things that are important.

When you work on something that's important to you, you feel that your days have meaning. When you just wander through life without a clear purpose, you feel like you're wasting your time. As Seneca once said, you want to make use of every day you're alive: "Let no one rob me of a single day who is not going to make me an adequate return for such a loss." To make sure no one can rob a day from you, do something meaningful every day. I can tell you from personal experience that nothing else motivates you like having a purpose.

When you do things that are meaningful, you never feel like you waste time. But when you feel like every day is the same, and you're not making any type of progress, you quickly get agitated. When that happens, take it as a sign to make a change.

But this doesn't have to be a giant life change. Change your mindset first. If other things require change, then so be it.

At least you're starting from the right place: Outside yourself. How can you do something that's useful to others? Ask yourself that question every time you're stuck, and you will never be in that position for long. Good things come when we look to make an impact.

LETTER 66:
ON BECOMING UNSTOPPABLE

What do you do when you don't get something you really want? I'm talking about both small things and big things. I used to get discouraged every time I experienced some sort of pushback or friction.

When I was in college, I would often get frustrated when we had to do group assignments and one of the group members didn't show up. For some classes, you couldn't choose who you would team up with. The professors would put people together randomly. As far as I can remember, there was always one odd person in the group, someone who wouldn't keep their word or would do sloppy work. The rest of the group would accept it and just do the work for the slacker. I did that as well. But here's the problem.

The way you treat small problems becomes how you treat big ones.

This is something I learned from the Stoics. They were steadfast people who took pride in being unstoppable. If they decided to do something–anything–they committed to doing it well.

Epictetus said it best: "When you decide to do something you believe to be right, don't let others stop you, even if a majority of people disapprove of it. If it is the wrong thing to do, you should not do it in the first place. But if it is the right thing, then why care about what others think?" The right thing to do when someone is slacking is to confront them and tell them they are not holding up their end of the bargain. You can always offer people a chance to change. But at some point, we must draw the line. This applies beyond class projects, of course, into our professional and everyday lives. Here's another small example. When I was in Spain a few weeks ago, I rented a car from Sixt, a German rental company. I paid for the car in advance, and they took a €300 deposit. When I handed in the car, they didn't give me back the deposit. They said I should receive it back automatically in a few days. When that didn't happen, I contacted them. But their customer service was really bad. I called them and the person said he couldn't help.

So I emailed them. A week went by... no response. I said to myself, "I'm getting my deposit back, no matter what." I found email addresses from their offices in The Netherlands and Germany. I emailed them and finally got a response from their Dutch office: "Ok, we'll take care of this. You'll get your deposit back." I confirmed my bank account with them and waited to get my money back. A few days go by, no response. I emailed their offices again. I emailed them every single day for five days. I said to myself, "I will not stop until I get my money back." That day, I got my money back.

I'm talking about small examples because it's easy to say, "Oh, it's just a small thing, I'll let it slide" No, it's not! It's about how you respond to things in life. If you know you're doing the right thing, don't let anyone stop you.

This is an important lesson about life. It's the same thing with working out. One of my favorite sports commentators is Skip Bayless, the host of Undisputed. He's 70 years old, and he's on TV every day for his 2.5 hours show. To stay in shape, he works out every day. And his motto is: "Never miss." He learned that when you miss one day, you're more inclined to miss another, and then another. Same thing with how you act.

If you let one little thing slip, you'll let more things slip. Before you know it, you let everything slip.

Now, this mindset is great for dealing with challenges or at work. It's not appropriate for relationships or when it comes to mental health. Of course, you don't want to be unforgiving and exacting in your personal life. That's the recipe for becoming an annoying person. But chances are, you want to become unstoppable outside the home. That's something I learned from my mom. She always said, "At home, be nice to everyone. Outside of the house, kick everyone's ass."

LETTER 67:
ON PERSONAL POWER
AND OWNERSHIP

When you watch the news, you think the world is about to end. Honestly, if you consume the news on any given day of the year, you're confronted with so many big world problems that you can't help but think, "The world is getting worse."

I see this with a lot of my family members as well. They are addicted to watching the news, and it puts them in a perpetually fearful mindset. What about inflation? What about wars? What about food shortages? What about evil governments?

I've noticed that people who consume a lot of news become passive. They look at others for the answers.

They want everybody else to solve their problems. But here's the thing, there have always been big challenges in life. I'm currently writing my next book, which is about applying Stoicism to investing. Part of my research is to look at previous stock market collapses. I've been reading a lot of newspaper articles from early 2009 when sentiment about the economy and the world was at historical lows. In a WSJ article, an economist warned people of an impending depression: "There's no way we are going to be able to avert a deep and long recession." Well, that was the time that things slowly started to improve again. By June 2009, the US was officially out of a recession. Things always seem way worse when we're at the bottom of a crisis. As I'm writing this, I'm seeing more and more of the same type of content you saw in 2008 and 2009, which was all about the financial crisis. For months, many economists and experts feared the worst. Unemployment was rising, profits were falling, and growth outlooks were getting slashed. People warned of a much slower economy. Banks would be stricter and access to capital would be way harder.

Just a year later, the economy started to improve, and the stock market went on a tear. Always remember that we don't have control over what we see on the news. Everything they talk about is macro news. Everybody knows that a single person can't control the economy or politics. We only control our own actions and judgments.

As Epictetus said, your goal in life is to:
"Make the best use of what is in your power,
and take the rest as it happens."

Every day, we must remind ourselves that we have power over our actions. With that power comes responsibility. If we waste our time and energy on activities that don't improve our lives, it's on us. Stoics never blame others for what's going on in their lives. If we're out of shape, low on energy, and lackluster about life, that's because we didn't make the best use of our time and energy. Some people don't agree with that and prefer to keep blaming others. Let them. What others do is none of our business. Let us commit to making the best of any situation. Let's focus on the things that are within our control. And let's make those things we control better.

LETTER 68:
ON BEING A FRIEND
TO YOURSELF

Do you treat your friends better than you treat yourself? When a friend screws something up, you probably say, "Don't be too hard on yourself." But what do you say to yourself in a similar situation?

Our self-talk is often much more critical than the way we would talk to a friend. I used to be like that. If I made the smallest mistake, like forgetting to close a window or something dumb like that, I would say, "This is really stupid. How can you forget to close your window? Well, say goodbye to your stuff. Someone will steal everything."

The weird thing is that we're often relaxed in our interactions with friends or co-workers, but supercritical the closer people become to us. The way we treat others (and ourselves) looks something like this:

- Strangers and acquaintances: Polite behavior, but other than that distant because we don't know them.

- Friends and co-workers: Polite and helpful behavior, trying to support them.

- Family, partner, children: More critical of them because we assume they will take everything.

- Self: All kinds of behavior, from being critical to aggressive towards ourselves.

We need to flip this whole dynamic. Let's treat ourselves the way we treat our friends. And let's do the same with our loved ones. It's something I'm constantly working on as someone who's naturally critical.

When Seneca was talking about the progress he made as a human being, he said: "What progress, you ask, have I made? I have begun to be a friend to myself."

Think about the importance of this concept. Seneca could've said anything that was related to self-improvement or Stoicism. Why didn't he say something like, "I have begun to focus on what I control"? That would be perfectly logical because that's the first lesson of Stoicism. I take Seneca's answer as a sign that being a friend to yourself might be one of the most important things in life. It's so true.

Out of all the people in the world, you spend the most time with yourself. Why treat yourself as anything other than a true friend? The beauty of treating yourself well is that it also rubs off on the way you treat others. This is the biggest thing I've experienced from living by this strategy. The less critical I've become of myself over the years, the more relaxed I've become in my relationships with others.

Seneca was also on to this; he said that "he who is a friend to himself is a friend to all mankind." I used to be the type who would analyze everything my partner said. "Why did you say that" and "why did you do that" were my favorite phrases. When you consistently ask that about other people, it means you can't understand why someone would do things differently than the way you think is right. But the rest of the world doesn't need to hold themselves to your standards. This is why friendships are usually great. When you're friends, you don't try to force your beliefs, habits, and ideas down your friend's throat. You just let them be. What's more, most of us even admire some of the quirky traits of our friends. We all have a friend who always shows up late to social engagements. Most of us turn it into an inside joke and laugh when the friend finally shows up. But we don't cut ourselves some slack when it comes to small things.

Who cares if you made a mistake?
Allow yourself to fall. Just stand up again!

Who cares if your partner or family member isn't in a great mood? Just let them be. Or better yet, do something fun to cheer them up. And if it doesn't work, that's fine too.

We can all use some more patience, with ourselves and others. Next time you're being critical of yourself, remind yourself to be a friend... to yourself.

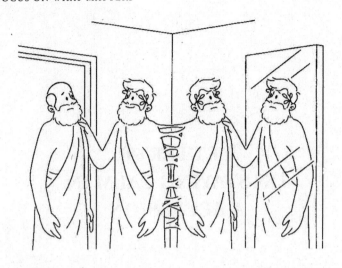

LETTER 69:
ON STAYING CALM IN
A RECESSION

You're probably hearing about it every day: Inflation is still high, stocks are down, companies have stopped hiring and some have even initiated layoffs. Many factors play roles when it comes to the economy and growth. The problem is that individuals tend to take a very up-close view of the issue. To really understand what's going on, we need a broader perspective. For example:

- **Up-close view:** Looking at inflation, interest rates, debt, consumer spending, joblessness, and so forth

- **Broad view:** Looking at long-term trends and historical patterns

As the platitude goes: History doesn't repeat, it rhymes. What happened in the last 100 years can teach us lessons about what's happening now. Historically, we've gone through periods of high growth, and periods of low growth, or contraction. Howard Marks, a very famous investor, wrote a book about this called *Mastering The Market Cycle*. The book discusses how the economy historically has grown at a steady pace, on average. But there were many years when growth was higher, and years it was lower.

That's because there's a cycle. The economy gets stimulated by the government (like in 2020), people get excited, take more risks, start to consume more, which causes inflation, and after this keeps going up, everything slows down again.

We might get a recession or just a slowdown. We go back to lower growth or contraction. This is not a bad process... unless you took on too much risk during the boom. Think of the people who bought houses without income in the 2000s.

Or the people who bought stocks and crypto with borrowed money over the last year.

During recessions, it's not like the world ends. It's just a slowdown. My father and I started our company during the Great Recession, which took a lot longer in Europe than in the US. It might've been really bad on the whole, but individual people kept moving forward. Sure, companies and people spent less. There were many jobs lost. Companies went under. But isn't that a part of a healthy economy? This is such an obvious thing to say, but the economy goes up and down. It's a fact of life.

We all want that prosperous times never end and the economy goes up in a straight line. But that's not what has happened historically. We should accept reality, no matter how hard it is. Epictetus put it best when he said:

"Do not seek to have events happen as you want them but instead want them to happen and your life will go well."

The good thing about the economy is that unlike a company or a person, it never dies. Like Marks says in his book, it's a cycle that keeps moving. Up and down, up and down.

A great way to see the evidence of this is to look at the historical returns of the S&P500. Stocks went up really fast during the 50s and 60s, came down in the 70s, went up in the 80s and 90s, and came down hard in the 2000s. On average, we've still had 10 per cent annualized returns.

It's easy to let your emotions take over: "This inflation will never end, currencies are going bust, the west is declining, there's war in Europe, we're next, people are getting crazier." I do agree that life is always getting harder and more complex.

But we also have to be honest and stay calm: The past decade was relatively quiet. There were bad things, but not as bad as what people have gone through in the past. We just have to carry on. Gladly, many people in our economy have that mindset. That's what makes it unbreakable.

LETTER 70:
ON THE IMPERMANENT
NATURE OF YOUR BODY

The other day, I was watching an interview with Khabib Nurmagomedov. He's a retired Mixed Martial Arts fighter who competed in the UFC, and many consider him as one of the best fighters/athletes of all time. I'm a big fan of his work ethic. Even now when he's retired, he trains just as hard as when he was competing. That's the philosophy he learned from his father, who passed away from complications due to Covid.

Khabib took the loss hard and it played into his decision to retire. He trained together with his father as a child, and he only took time off when he was injured. But he also kept training as long as his injuries weren't bad. The way Khabib trains, he's prone to getting injuries. As he once said: "My number one enemy is injuries because I train so hard."

If you randomly sample 100 high-level athletes like UFC fighters, NBA, or NFL players, you'll probably find that the majority of them are playing with some kind of small injury. Many athletes go through entire seasons with small pains and aches. This is the condition of the human body. Even if you're not an elite athlete, you probably always have something about your body that's aching—especially if you're past 30. The body starts breaking down faster every single year we're alive. I'm only 34 and I always have something that doesn't feel 100 per cent in my body. Right now, it's my right foot, which has been bugging me on and off for the past year. Last week, it was my stomach. And if we're not experiencing injuries, we see our bodies changing over the years. Our hair turns gray, will thin out. We get wrinkles. You know, the normal aging stuff. So many people freak out and try everything to stop the aging process. Not the Stoics. They practiced the same detachment they applied to external factors like the weather to their bodies.

To them, you couldn't get attached to anything—not even your own body. Seneca explained why that's important: "I acknowledge that affection for our body is innate in us, and I acknowledge that we are its guardians and protectors. I don't deny that I should indulge it, only that I should be enslaved to it. For the man who is a slave to his body, who is too afraid for it, who relates all actions to its needs, will also be a slave to many people."

When you're afraid of losing your youthful appearance, you can become a slave to your body.

But if you have the ability and strength to distance yourself from your body and acknowledge its impermanent nature, you will be free. You will no longer get upset when you're injured because you realize that's the nature of life. Our bodies are subjected to illness and injuries, and sometimes there's nothing we can do but accept our predicament. The human body is fragile, and yet, it's surprisingly strong at the same time. You do have the power to heal yourself when it comes to most conditions that are not serious. Most of our injuries heal on their own, or with physical therapy. When we get the flu or a stomach virus, our body deals with the invaders on its own. But it can't avoid aging.

Acknowledging the impermanent nature of life is challenging, and sometimes can even feel scary, but it's also a good opportunity to practice Stoicism. Every time you're sick, injured, or see signs of aging, don't resist. See it as a reminder that everything with a beginning also has an end. We're born as tiny fragile creatures who grow into wonderful beings with sophisticated bodies, and gradually, we age. We can stay in shape and treat our bodies well, but there's a limit to how much we can do!

When we're sick, we should respect the signals our body sends us. When we age, we should be proud instead of trying to hide. This perspective shifts the anxiety of impermanence. We all prefer to be 24 for the rest of our lives, but time stops for nothing. That can be scary. But look at it this way: You will have a better life if you don't waste your energy on things you can't change. You don't want to be a slave to anything. You want to be free. So be free—of everything.

ACKNOWLEDGEMENTS

As always, a huge thank you to you. A writer is nothing without a reader. So thanks for reading this book until the end.

This column would not exist without the support of Jon Gluck, Michelle Woo, and Amy Shearn who were at Medium at the time I started this. They suggested the idea of writing a weekly column, which became the Stoic Letter. Nearly every letter (except for the last few) was edited by Amy, who I chatted with every week for nearly a year and a half. Without her input, the letters would lack depth, so Amy, thank you for that. In fact, shortly after Amy left Medium, I stopped writing the column because the solo writing process just didn't work.

Any type of endeavor, even the most alone centric like writing, requires some form of collaboration. In 2020, I hired John Pucay as my editor and researcher, who has provided valuable input on nearly every piece of content I've published. John also arranged the letters in this book into different categories. Thank you for that.

We don't always need a big team, but we do need teamwork to do better work.

All the best.

— Darius